AUTHENTICITY AMPLIFIED

How Real Leaders
Build Trust, Inspire Loyalty,
and **Get Results** That Last

MITCH HAYES

Special thanks to Ryan MacTaggart, PhD, for your support, advice, and work on this book.

First edition.

For my dad,

You're still my biggest advocate and my strongest supporter. Your belief gave me confidence, and your wisdom still shows up when I need it most.

I miss you like crazy—you're in everything I do.

This book is for you.

Contents

Foreword

by AK Schultz (CEO/Co-Founder SVT Robotics)

Many romanticize leadership as a noble pursuit—a realm of visionaries, change-makers, and trailblazers. But the truth is far less glamorous. I was honored when Mitch asked me to write the foreword for *Authenticity Amplified*, but I hesitated. Writing about leadership is not a simple task, especially when you've lived it long enough to understand its profound complexities. Yet, the essence of this book—authenticity in leadership—resonated with me. Leadership, at its core, is about embracing burdens and navigating decisions that are as tough as they are inevitable.

If your goal is to make friends or win popularity contests, leadership is not the path for you. True leadership is lonely and fraught with the weight of decisions that can never satisfy everyone. Every choice you make will have dissenters, critics who may think you're shortsighted, even foolish. The higher you rise, the more amplified these criticisms become.

Leadership is about more than making choices—it's about conviction, resilience, and adaptability. You need the courage to stand by your decisions while remaining open to pivot when the situation demands it. Leadership, in times of crisis, requires more than tactical skill; it calls for moral clarity. Figures like Abraham Lincoln and Winston Churchill faced unimaginable odds, often standing alone in their convictions. Their choices, while scrutinized and challenged in their time, have shaped history.

We remember leaders like them through a simplified lens, focusing on their triumphs while overlooking the grueling path they walked. Leadership in real time is messy, ambiguous, and, above all, human.

The Reality of Leadership

Leadership faces its greatest challenges in adversity. For instance, people often glamorize the startup world with images of foosball tables, meditation pods, and free sparkling water. Yet, true grit and resilience emerge when the "asteroid" hits—whether it's a market downturn, product failure, or many unforeseen challenges.

The truth about leadership is that it often feels thankless. If you lead long enough, you will face moments where your decisions hurt people—layoffs, product cancellations, or even the realization that someone on your team isn't the right fit. Avoiding these decisions out of fear or misplaced compassion can cause harm to the very team you're trying to protect. I call this the "asshole tax"—the cost of allowing under-performers or toxic individuals to stay, draining morale and productivity.

You must make tough decisions with empathy and clarity. Being inauthentic erodes trust and leaves teams rudderless. However, transparency, though uncomfortable, builds trust. People may disagree with your choices, but if they understand your reasoning and believe in your intent, they will respect you.

Authenticity in Action

Authenticity is not just a tool for good times; it's the bedrock of trust in turbulent moments. Leaders often sanitize tough decisions, using corporate jargon to avoid showing vulnerability. But people want to follow leaders who struggle, empathize, and care. Acknowledging how hard decisions weigh on you isn't a sign of weakness but rather a sign of humanity.

Authenticity doesn't mean perfection. Mistakes are inevitable. What sets influential leaders apart is their willingness to own their errors, learn from them, and move forward with humility. Leaders who hide their missteps, deflect blame, or attempt to maintain an image of infallibility lose credibility.

Lessons from the Front-line

Over my career—spanning military service, corporate management, and leading organizations—I've learned several truths about leadership:

---

1. **Trust is the Lubricant of Business:** Without trust, nothing moves. Teams stagnate, collaboration falters, and organizations crumble. We build trust through transparency, consistent action, and a genuine investment in others' well-being.

---

2. **People Want to Join a Cause, Not Just a Company:** Purpose drives engagement. Employees want to be part of something bigger than themselves. An interesting vision inspires loyalty and perseverance, even during difficult times.

---

3. **Bold Goals Require Bite-Sized Plans:** Dream big but execute small. Break ambitious objectives into manageable chunks to keep teams motivated and focused.

---

4. **Vulnerability Builds Connection:** Leaders who admit their struggles and show empathy foster deeper connections. Being vulnerable doesn't diminish authority—it enhances it.

---

5. **The Moral High Ground is a Choice:** Leadership is not just about legality or profitability but also about doing what's right,

even when it's not popular or convenient. Decisions rooted in morality inspire trust and loyalty.

6. **Action Over Perfection:** Indecision is a silent killer. While being decisive carries risks, failing to act guarantees stagnation. Leaders must cultivate a bias toward action.

7. **Celebrate True Wins, Not Participation Trophies:** Empty celebrations erode credibility. Recognize meaningful achievements and maintain high standards to foster a culture of excellence.

8. **Lead with Humanity, Even in Hard Times:** Whether it's a layoff or a major pivot, how you handle tough moments defines you as a leader. Compassion, honesty, and respect go a long way in preserving trust and morale.

Becoming a Better Leader

Leadership is not a destination, but a journey of constant learning. Surround yourself with people smarter than you in their respective fields and embrace the vulnerability this requires. Empowering others doesn't diminish your authority—it magnifies your impact. Influential leaders create environments where others thrive and grow, even surpassing them.

Above all, remember that leadership is not about you. It's about the team, the mission, and the legacy you leave behind. Success, when built on authenticity, is more than a financial gain. It's the pride of mentoring others, the satisfaction of building something meaningful, and the knowledge that you've led with integrity.

Leadership is hard. It's lonely, challenging, and heartbreaking. But it's also one of the most rewarding paths you can walk. If you lead with authenticity, you'll inspire not just results but trust, respect, and lasting impact.

Authenticity Amplified: Unleashing Your Leadership Potential delves deeper into these principles, offering a road map for leaders who strive to differ. It's a guide for those who understand that leadership is not about perfection but about being human—and amplifying that humanity in every decision, every interaction, and every moment.

Introduction

An Evolution of Leadership: From Authority to Authenticity

Imagine a leader stepping into the office wearing mismatched socks and a coffee-stained shirt, not because she's trying to make a point, but because that's just who she is. Her focus is on what matters, not appearances. The team chuckles, relaxes, and gets down to business quickly because they know what to expect from her. They really know her. There's no facade, no pretense—just a sense of trust and a connection that inspires everyone to bring their best to the team.

In contrast, consider a charismatic leader; his energy is palpable, a vibrant force that instantly commands respect and focus. He captivates everyone effortlessly with his polished, confident, and magnetic presence. Initially, he appears to be the perfect leader. Charisma can energize a room and inspire people to support a vision, but charisma alone does not get the job done when leading people. If his words do not match his actions, if his charm seems rehearsed and his promises hollow, the initial excitement fades. Teams grow tired of the "same old song and dance" and question whether their leader is genuine or just pretending.

We've all encountered both types of leaders. The charismatic leader may dazzle but leaves you wondering whether you can rely on them. On the other hand, the authentic leader who makes you feel seen, heard, and valued, creates the environment where trust flourishes, ideas flow freely, and people feel empowered to take risks. Charisma might get people to listen, but authenticity makes them believe.

The leader with mismatched socks matters because her power comes from trust, not just charisma. Authenticity, not perfection, inspires confidence in her leadership. Authentic leaders admit they don't have all the answers but trust the group to figure things out together. They earn respect by showing up as their true selves, not by projecting perfection.

For so long, we've idolized a version of leadership defined by perfection—an image of the untouchable leader, polished and infallible. We expected leaders to have all the answers, issue orders without hesitation, and project unwavering control. That style of leadership served its purpose in the industrial age, when rigid systems demanded obedience and efficiency. Times have changed. The people we lead have changed too.

In today's interconnected, complex, and collaborative world, being present is crucial. People want someone who will stand by their side, listen, learn, and adapt. They want a leader who can admit fallibility and be committed to collaborative problem-solving. Authentic leaders strive to build bridges while perfect leaders always seem distant from their teams.

In 2015, I was a Project Manager and felt stuck in my career. I couldn't figure out why. I had done all the right things. I was a disciple of Jim Collin's *Good to Great* and wholeheartedly believed in Level 5 Leadership, the Hedgehog Concept, and discipline. But something wasn't clicking and I felt a disconnection.

One rainy "Casual Friday" morning while getting ready, I realized my only pair of jeans was in the wash, and I didn't feel like putting on dress shoes. I knew I had a busy day ahead of me and instead of focusing on my team and the tasks at hand, I was contemplating what to wear. Seriously? I remember thinking, "Screw it. My team needs me at my best today." I wore a pair of running pants, running shoes, a long-sleeved T-shirt and a vest to work. Not sloppy, but comfortable. I can distinctly remember some of the decision we made that day.

The truth was, up until that day I didn't let people in. I kept my work and personal life separate. I wasn't hiding anything; I simply thought that's how it was supposed to be. I thought being a leader required remaining polished and professional at all times. Never let your guard down, right?

But I realized that the people I trusted most at work were those I knew on a personal level. I figured if people got to know the real me, then maybe they'd trust me as a leader, too. I made it a priority to show up as myself and get to know the people around me on a more personal level. I started bringing people into decisions that affected them. I cared more about what people's opinions were and took their suggestions under advisement. I listened more. I started making decisions based on people instead of profit, but somehow this new model was improving all the metrics I was accountable for.

A distinct shift had occurred in how I was leading and everyone was taking note. I moved from managing a small team of project managers, to managing a larger department team. I was asked to lead a struggling sales and consulting team and then was given the opportunity to collaborate with teams all over the world. It all became "real" when I was asked to lead the division I had joined just five years earlier. Over the next few years, we turned around our division that historically struggled with high turnover rates and less than desirable financial results into a culture forward, profitable unit once again.

In 2021, after realizing the company was not fully onboard with where I wanted to take the division next, I took a leap. It was time for me to put my leadership theories to the ultimate test. I accepted the opportunity to start a new division in the U.S. for a global automation company. Six years after I showed up to work in running pant for the first time as a stalled-out

Project Manager, I was the President of a new company and leading in a way that felt like *me*.

Since launching the division in August 2021, we've grown to over $90M in new orders (2025) with a team of 100+ people. We became profitable in less than 4 years. More than 35% of our new team members have come through existing team member referrals. Turnover is in the single digits. Over 15% of our team members are people I've worked with before, including the first Project Manager on my team back in 2015 and a former boss. They both are part of my current leadership team (and show up in stories in this book).

We've built a culture rooted in trust, transparency, and people knowing exactly who they're working with. I've had the chance to work with customers and partners across North America, Europe, Australia, and Southeast Asia. The relationships I've cultivated are built on mutual respect. I take the time to understand who people are, and they always know who I am and where I stand.

This book comes straight from my journey from trying to be the perfect leader to building something real. *Authenticity Amplified* is for anyone who's tired of leadership advice that skips the human part.

Over the past few years, I've shared this same message about real leadership, personal growth, and the things that build trust on LinkedIn. My audience has a global reach, and the engagement I get each week continues to reinforce what I've seen firsthand: people are hungry for leadership that's honest, relatable, and real.

There's no shortage of leadership books. You can find hundreds on vision, performance, discipline, and habits. Some are polished and academic. Others lean hard into military principles or self-help playbooks. Many of them are good, I read a lot of them still. But most of them skip the part about being authentic. Authenticity wasn't in any leadership book I had ever read.

Books like *Leaders Eat Last*, *Radical Candor*, and *Extreme Ownership* offer something useful. But most of them ask you to adopt a complete system. In theory, that sounds great, but a complete step-by-step system rarely works. You read a book like that and realize maybe half of it applies to your world. You're left wondering if any of it will work if you can't apply it all. That's the problem with most leadership frameworks: they're built as all-or-nothing systems. And real leadership doesn't work like that.

Authenticity Amplified isn't a system or a script. It's a way of leading that starts with knowing yourself and being seen. It's about building real trust by showing up consistently, communicating clearly, and staying grounded in what matters. These are all things we know, but we forget to put into practice on a daily basis.

This book walks through how to build a culture rooted in trust and transparency, what leading by example really means, how to communicate with clarity and conviction, especially in tough moments, and how to create an environment where people feel known and want to do their best work. It also digs into the moments most books gloss over — situations such as when leadership starts to feel heavy, or you catch yourself drifting away from the people and values that matter most.

I went from a stalled-out project manager to the president of a fast-growing business by learning how to lead without pretending. I don't get it right all the time and neither will you, but we don't have to either. I've built a team and a culture that works because people trust who I am and know where I stand.

The world doesn't require additional leaders who feign perfection. What it needs are leaders that embody authenticity. Consider those who shaped your life, professionally or personally. The most impressive resume or the most polished presenter didn't come to your mind but a person who really connected with you on a personal level did. Maybe it was a manager who admitted they had struggled with the same challenge you were facing and offered to help you navigate the problem and a solution. Perhaps a mentor recognized your potential when you couldn't see the path. Perhaps a leader, confronting adversity, eschewed corporate jargon and instead offered direct, truthful communication. Those are the leaders we remember. Their humanity mattered more than their perfection. This book is full of those people I remember.

In a world obsessed with appearances, authenticity feels rare. Social media bombards us with curated versions of success and highlight reels that hide the messiness and effort behind the scenes. Companies often use meaningless phrases like *innovative* and *cutting-edge* to describe their products. It's easy to become cynical. We crave something real, something we can trust. This is where authentic leadership stands apart. It cuts through the noise and says, *"Here I am. This is what I believe. Let's figure it out together."*

But what defines an authentic leader?

Being an authentic leader means aligning who you are with how you lead. It doesn't mean oversharing every detail of your life or admitting your every insecurity. Honest self-assessment reveals areas of strength and of needed improvement. Authentic leaders listen more than they speak, learn more than they teach, and show up for the people they lead, not as an idealized version of a leader but as a real, imperfect, developing self. And it takes courage. The courage to go against the perceived rules of leadership, which are antiquated and ready for a shift.

The Fall of "Perfect" Leadership

Up until recently, the ultimate aim of perfect leadership has been to always be confident and unwavering and never showing vulnerability or weakness. Such leadership stems from prioritizing certainty, efficiency, and results above curiosity, connection, and relationships.

But what happens when a leader never admits they're wrong? What happens when they never share their challenges or uncertainties?

First, trust breaks down or is never established to begin with. Teams become afraid to speak up or take risks. People fear failure more than they crave innovation, which stifles creativity. The leader, despite their best intentions, becomes isolated and cut off from the insights, questions, and feedback that could make them better.

I worked on a project several years ago for a customer that centered every project and product around the idea that dreams can come true, magic is real, and fairy-tales have happy endings. The Project Manager leading the team for the client had an email signature that read, *"I don't believe in miracles, I expect them."* Every email message she sent ended with that signature. At first, I thought it was a playful nod to the company's culture, but I quickly realized her signature wasn't playful at all—it was a warning.

"Failure," she explained to us during one of our early conversations, "isn't just frowned upon here. It's unacceptable." And she meant it. She never admitted mistakes, never showed uncertainty, and never asked a question she didn't already have the answer. On the surface, she appeared confident, polished, and entirely in control. But our team saw things differently.

The collective group rarely shared ideas because they feared being wrong. They stopped taking risks because failure wasn't an option. They consistently came to work, but they left their creativity, curiosity, and humanity at home.

The company culture worshiped perfection, but at a cost. The relentless demand for miracles created a workplace where trust, innovation, and growth were all but impossible. The irony was obvious. In a company designed to produce magic, the fear of failure had stifled the joy and freedom of the employees who created it.

Perfection breeds fear instead of inspiring trust. To achieve success, we need an environment that promotes collaboration, innovation, and growth. This environment should be fearless. Real miracles in the business world don't come from perfection but from leaders and teams that have trust, transparency, and the courage to embrace imperfection.

The most successful leaders today are those unafraid to challenge norms. They are the leaders who proudly say, "I don't know, but I'm open to learning." They understand the importance of building strong relationships, alongside achieving desired outcomes. Instead of perceiving vulnerability as a weakness, they recognize it as a source of strength.

Authenticity is Hard—and So Necessary

Embracing authenticity isn't easy. It requires stepping into uncertainty and asking yourself hard questions: *Who am I as a leader? What values guide me? Where do I refrain because of the fear of being judged?* Authenticity means being honest not just with others but with yourself.

For many leaders, that's a terrifying prospect. Vulnerability feels risky. What if people lose respect for me? What if admitting a mistake makes me look weak? But here's the truth: vulnerability is what builds trust.

Admitting failure sends a powerful message that *It's safe to try, safe to fail, and safe to learn.* A leader asking for help shows that collaboration isn't just encouraged but expected. Authentic leadership empowers others and creates permission for others to do the same.

The Impact of Authentic Leadership

Authenticity doesn't lower the bar or sacrifice results; it does the opposite. Leaders who embrace authenticity create environments where trust flourishes. Those around you feel empowered to contribute their ideas, and teams tackle challenges with resilience and creativity.

Authenticity inspires commitment because it builds connection and drives innovation by creating safety and unlocking the potential of the people you lead, giving them permission to show up fully as themselves.

If you've ever felt the pressure to be someone you're not and hide your struggles, avoid tough conversations, or pretend you're always in control, you're not alone. That pressure is real, but also unnecessary. The most effective leaders listen more than they speak, learn more than they teach, and inspire others by showing up as themselves.

Research shows the profound impact of authentic leadership on employee engagement and organizational success. A study published in *Industrial and Commercial Training*, based on a survey of 245 employees, found that authentic leadership was positively and significantly associated with employee engagement, with the work environment partially mediating this relationship (Dartey-Baah et al., 2024). Another study reported that authentic leadership and strong employee–organization relationships together explained approximately 68.8 % of the variance in employee engagement outcomes in an organizational setting (Ramadhan, 2025)

Beyond engagement, authentic leadership enhances individual and team performance. Research in *Frontiers in Psychology* found that when leaders embrace vulnerability and foster open dialogue, they unlock their team's potential (Rego et al., 2012). Employees in such environments are more likely to share ideas, take calculated risks, and adapt to challenges creatively. Authenticity is about leading with integrity while encouraging innovation and resilience.

These findings are reminders that connection, not perfection, is the goal. Leadership rooted in authenticity creates a ripple effect. Teams follow suit, building cultures where trust and transparency become the norm. As Brené Brown says, "Vulnerability is not winning or losing; it's having the courage to show up when you can't control the outcome" (Brown, 2018).

Imagine starting a meeting with, "I made a mistake last quarter, and here's what I've learned. I'd love your input on our next steps." It's a simple yet powerful gesture that transforms a group of employees into a collaborative team.

Authenticity is a commitment to integrity, courage, and a genuine desire to connect and recognize that the path to meaningful leadership doesn't lie in perfection, but in the ability to inspire trust, foster collaboration, and navigate challenges alongside your team.

Authentic leaders don't just influence outcomes, they transform cultures.

Leadership today isn't about standing above, rather, it's about standing with. It's about creating environments where people feel empowered to contribute, innovate, and grow. By committing to authenticity, you're not only unlocking your own potential, but you're also inspiring others to do the same.

Embrace your unique leadership journey. Throughout this book, we will explore how authenticity can amplify your impact, strengthen relationships, and inspire others. You will gain tools to lead with confidence and purpose through real-world examples, actionable strategies, and honest reflections.

This book is for anyone tired of leadership advice that feels disconnected from real life. It's not about trying to be someone else. It's time to figure out how to lead as yourself and make that your biggest strength.

The world doesn't need perfect leaders. It needs leaders who are willing to step into the messiness of life with courage and grace. Are you ready to come join us?

1

Defining Authentic Leadership

When you think about an inspiring leader, what comes to mind? Is it their ability to make tough decisions, their strategic thinking, or maybe their knack for rallying a team around a common goal? These qualities are undeniably important, but there's one element that ties them all together: authenticity. Authenticity is the keystone that holds the arch of influence and inspiration together. It's what sets exceptional leaders apart from those who are merely competent, allowing them to connect deeply with their teams, inspire unwavering loyalty, and drive remarkable results.

But authenticity in leadership isn't just a personality trait or communication style. It's a choice leaders must make every day, especially when the pressure is on and the easy path conflicts with their values. And that choice has consequences far beyond the individual leader.

Authenticity is not a passive trait—it's a deliberate decision made repeatedly in the face of pressure. Every leader will face these decision points. Do you compromise your values for an easier path? Or do you lean into authenticity, knowing the path might take longer or be more difficult?

Authentic leadership is not just about personal integrity—it has a profound effect on organizations and the people within them. Leaders who embrace authenticity shape company culture, foster trust, and set new standards for their industry. Their influence extends beyond their immediate teams and ripples through the entire organization, creating long-lasting benefits that outlive their tenure.

Authentic leadership proves even more essential in today's rapidly evolving business world. We live in an era of constant technological change. Our global workforce is both more connected and diverse. We have a heightened awareness of social and environmental issues. These complexities increasingly demand leaders navigate uncertainty and inspire trust through authenticity.

Remember when a leader inspired you. Did they inspire by having all the right answers or something else? Perhaps it was their openness during a tough situation or how they made you feel appreciated and heard. We rarely remember the leaders who had all the answers all the time, which isn't inspiring at all. We don't care if they were perfect, but we remember if they were genuine. Inspirational leaders take time to understand both themselves and their teams, clarify their values, and lead in a way that aligns with those beliefs. They are true to themselves during challenging times and foster a safe space for others to do the same.

Modern life prompts constant questioning concerning truth versus falsehood. Is that image we saw online a genuine photo, or is it digitally manipulated? Are we speaking to a real person on the phone, or is it an AI chat-bot? In a world filled with polished facades and digital illusions, authenticity stands out. People are tired of corporate jargon, empty promises, and leaders who seem out of touch with the realities of their teams and customers. We need leaders who are transparent, admit their shortcomings, and strive to make a difference.

Remote work and digital communication growth have increased this demand. When we're no longer sharing physical spaces, it's easy for trust and connection to dissipate. Authentic leaders bridge that gap by being present and genuine, whether through a Zoom call or an email, because they understand the message impact hinges on both delivery and intent.

Reflect on your own leadership journey. When have you felt most connected to your team or organization? When have you been most proud of your leadership? It is likely when you were genuine, leading with your values, and unconstrained by leadership stereotypes.

Consider how authenticity plays a role in your own leadership style. How can you bring more of your true self into your leadership? How can you create a space where others feel empowered to do the same? Because in the end, authentic leadership isn't just good for business—it's what makes leadership meaningful.

The Essence of Authenticity in Leadership

Authentic leadership is about knowing who you are, from your strengths and struggles, to your values, and life stories. It is leading with honesty and heart. It's showing that you're relatable and can be vulnerable, building the kind of trust that sticks, even when things get tough.

Vulnerability might be one of the hardest aspects of authentic leadership. Typically, we expect leaders to have everything figured out and to be strong, unwavering pillars of certainty. But actual strength comes from showing your humanity by acknowledging fallibility, admitting errors, and fostering a secure environment for team members.

Picture a time when your team faced unforeseen difficulties: deadlines slipping, team spirit unraveling, and frustration. Tension lingers heavy and unspoken. How did your leader respond? Did they mask the chaos with forced confidence, their control appearing brittle? Or did they choose authenticity and acknowledge the challenges openly and honestly? Authentic leadership isn't about projecting endless positivity; it's about recognizing struggles and facing them head-on, even when it's uncomfortable.

Being authentic is about being honest about the things that matter including your vision, concerns, and aspirations for the team, which can be done without oversharing or confessing insecurity. Being honest shows your team that you trust them enough to be genuine, and you're willing to listen and learn from their insights.

This kind of leadership builds trust and fosters collaboration. Team members seeing their leader embracing vulnerability encourages them to also show up as their true selves, which fosters a culture that values intrinsic worth alongside contributions. Real innovation and progress begin when teams feel empowered to take risks, share bold ideas, and strive for more than they thought possible.

One of the most inspiring examples I've seen comes from a colleague who despite leading a highly successful team, wasn't afraid to admit when he didn't know something. He would openly ask team members to take the lead in areas where they had more expertise, saying things like, "I'm not the best at this. Can you show us the way?" Watching the team's response was powerful. People not only stepped up to the challenge, but their respect and loyalty for him grew immensely. His vulnerability showed that asking for help is a testament to his confidence in his team, not a sign of weakness.

In my career, I have struggled with business development, the "in between" of marketing and sales. Marketing generated leads but turning those leads into opportunities felt impossible. I could sell and close deals, but nurturing leads was a different story. After months of trying to figure things out alone, I realized I needed help. I asked my team, "How can we change our approach to convert these leads?"

That moment of vulnerability was transformative. Not only did my team come together to create a successful strategy, but they saw that I trusted and valued their expertise. The result? Our pipeline grew stronger, and we turned those leads into sales. Admitting I didn't have all the answers was a turning point, not just for the team, but for me as a leader. Asking for input reinforced that leading authentically means embracing your limitations and celebrating the strengths of those around you.

Authentic leaders don't focus on maintaining a flawless image. They're committed to something bigger than themselves. Their willingness to say,

"I don't know, but I'm willing to learn," or "I was wrong, and I'm ready to correct it," is apparent. When leaders are open and genuine, they create a culture where trust and respect thrive.

So, ask yourself: When was the last time you asked for help from a mentor, a peer, or your own team? Leadership is about knowing when to seek support and acknowledging that each person has something valuable to contribute. Have you noticed that the most vulnerable leaders are often the ones most committed to a cause greater than themselves? It's not a coincidence. By embracing your own vulnerability, you're showing your team that you're in this together, which conveys you're all part of something meaningful and worthwhile.

The Cornerstones of Authentic Leadership

Just as a house relies on its cornerstones for strength and stability, your leadership rests on a few essential principles that support everything you do. These cornerstones of self-awareness, transparency, integrity, and consistency aren't just concepts to understand; they're the foundation you build upon, day in and day out.

Without a solid foundation, a house becomes unstable. If even one cornerstone is weak or out of alignment, the entire structure is at risk. The same goes for leadership. Unless you're fully aware of your strengths *and* weaknesses, your actions may seem disjointed or insincere. If you're not transparent, trust breaks down quickly. If you lack integrity, your credibility crumbles. Without consistency, your leadership becomes unpredictable, leaving your team unsure of what to expect.

These cornerstones are part of who you are. You don't have to build them from scratch, but you do need to reinforce them regularly. You've likely encountered these ideas in books or discussions but knowing about them and actively practicing them are two different things. Agreeing with the concept of self-awareness or transparency is easy, embodying these values consistently, especially under pressure, is much more difficult.

As we explore each cornerstone, I encourage you to think about your own leadership foundation. Where are your areas of strength? Where do you need reinforcement? How can you align and solidify all four cornerstones to ensure your leadership remains resilient in challenging times?

Here's a quick look at each cornerstone:

1. **Self-Awareness:** Understanding your strengths, weaknesses, and what drives you.
2. **Transparency:** Building trust through openness and honesty in your communications.
3. **Integrity:** Aligning your actions with your values, even when it's difficult.
4. **Consistency:** Providing stability and reliability in your leadership so your team knows they can count on you.

Like a table with four legs, these principles hold your leadership up and give it structure. If any one of them falters, the strength of your leadership weakens. As we dive deeper into each cornerstone, think about how you can strengthen your foundation to build a leadership legacy that's not just impactful, but unshakable.

Self-Awareness: The First Cornerstone of Authentic Leadership

Self-awareness is where authentic leadership truly begins. It's about understanding yourself at the deepest level. Know your values, beliefs, and emotional triggers, and recognize how they influence your decisions and interactions. Without this foundational knowledge, leading authentically is challenging because you're not fully in touch with whom you are at your core.

Developing self-awareness requires an ongoing commitment to reflection and a willingness to face uncomfortable truths.

Start by asking yourself some tough questions:

What are my core values?

What drives my decisions?

How do my actions reflect my beliefs?

Where do I struggle, and how can I improve?

Keeping a leadership journal can be an invaluable tool, allowing you to track your growth over time and gain deeper insights into your leadership style. Be honest about your strengths and limitations. Understand how self-awareness shapes your perceptions. It's not just about introspection, but how using the insight gained allows you to lead more effectively and align your actions.

Another essential aspect of self-awareness is seeking honest feedback from others. This can be challenging, as it requires you to be open to criticism and willing to change. Asking for feedback is crucial for growth. Ask your team, peers, and family for their perspectives on your leadership. What are your strengths? Where could you improve? How do they experience your leadership? These conversations, though sometimes uncomfortable, can provide a clearer picture of your impact and help you identify areas for development.

The goal is to cultivate awareness to understand how your behavior affects those around you and being willing to adjust when necessary. This kind of self-awareness is one of the cornerstones of authentic leadership, enabling you to lead with intention, integrity, and a genuine connection to your team.

Transparency: The Second Cornerstone of Authentic Leadership

Transparency is about creating a culture where honesty, openness, and trust are the norm. It is about sharing your thought processes, challenges, and even uncertainties with your team. When you're transparent, you invite others to do the same, building trust and respect that strengthens every interaction.

One common fear among leaders is that transparency makes them appear vulnerable or unsure. However, transparency enhances your credibility by showing that you're confident enough to share the complete picture, not just the polished version. Think back to a time when you delivered tough news. Perhaps a project was delayed, or budget cuts were necessary. Did you try to soften the blow, or were you straightforward about the situation and its implications? The latter approach, while more challenging, is far more likely to build trust and respect because people prefer that you be transparent with them and respect leaders who don't sugarcoat the situation.

Transparency doesn't mean sharing every detail with everyone. Instead, focus on communicating what's relevant, explaining the reasons behind your decisions, and being open to feedback. For instance, when facing a significant decision, I like to gather input by saying, "Imagine we're around a campfire, just sharing ideas. What are your thoughts?" This casual, open approach encourages honest dialogue and makes everyone feel valued and heard while allowing the opportunity to fully explain the situation.

Transparency also plays a vital role in managing uncertainty and change. It's best to be upfront when you don't have all the answers and involve your team in finding solutions. Whether you're acknowledging tough market conditions, discussing internal challenges, or simply admitting when you're unsure of the best path forward, being transparent transforms problems into shared goals.

Another critical aspect of transparency is having tough, sometimes uncomfortable conversations, whether you're providing constructive feedback, addressing performance issues, or discussing team misalignment. These conversations, though difficult, are essential for growth and improvement. I've found that when handled with empathy and focused on development, these conversations lead to positive outcomes for both the individual and the team. Sometimes, these discussions reveal that a team member isn't the right fit, but even then, transparency allows for a respectful and supportive transition. As a leader, transparency allows you to take responsibility, not only for the person's performance, but for the clarity and support they received from the team.

The goal of transparency is to build a culture where trust and open communication are the default. When people feel informed and included, they're more engaged and committed to the team's success. This trust creates a dynamic environment where collaboration thrives to achieve the organization's mission.

Remember, transparency is about creating a culture where feedback and ideas flow freely in all directions, not just top-down communication. Encourage your team to voice their opinions, ask questions, and share their perspectives. This two-way openness not only strengthens the organization's knowledge base but also fosters a sense of shared purpose and unity.

Adopting a transparent leadership style significantly influences the organizational culture by transforming it into one marked by openness, respect, and mutual support. This culture benefits not only internal team dynamics, but also the organization's reputation with clients, partners, and potential recruits. Embracing transparency requires courage and confidence and the willingness to be transparent is what sets truly authentic leaders apart. Being open about challenges, uncertainties, and your own vulnerabilities as a leader builds trust, strengthens relationships, and creates a resilient, cohesive organization. By adopting these qualities, leaders are better able to navigate the complexities of the modern business landscape with agility and confidence.

Connecting Self-Awareness and Transparency

Reflect on a recent decision or conversation where you needed to communicate something important to your team:

How did understanding your own values and beliefs influence what information you shared and how you shared it?

Were you clear about your intentions and reasoning?

If not, what could you have done differently to align your communication more closely with your core values?

Consider how practicing both self-awareness and transparency can enhance your leadership effectiveness and build trust within your team.

Integrity: The Third Cornerstone of Authentic Leadership

Integrity and ethics form the moral compass of authentic leadership. These are key elements that guide your decisions and actions, ensuring that you do what's right when doing so is difficult or unpopular. Leading with integrity means holding yourself accountable to the highest standards and standing by your principles, regardless of the personal cost.

One lesson I've learned over the years is that you can't fake integrity. It's not about crafting a polished statement of values to display on the wall. Integrity is how you show up every day, especially when no one is watching. At the organization where I'm fortunate enough to lead, we have a straightforward moral compass: if a decision would keep us up at night, we don't make it. A simple but powerful guideline. For me, staying true to our values and doing right by our clients and team members means being able to sleep soundly.

Have you ever been in a situation when doing the right thing came at a cost? Maybe you have faced pressure to overlook a problem to please a client, or you felt pressured to take shortcuts to meet a deadline. The choices you make in these moments reveal your true character as a leader. Integrity gives you the courage to stand firm, even when it's tempting to compromise. Make decisions you stand firmly behind, knowing that they reflect who you are and what you believe.

True integrity is about being consistent in showing up the same way with your team as you do with your clients, and upholding your values, no matter the circumstances to create a culture where honesty and ethical behavior aren't just encouraged but expected. When you set this standard, your team will follow your lead, and together you'll build an environment where trust and respect thrive.

There's a saying I always go back to: "If you don't have integrity, you have nothing." Without integrity, everything else falls apart. People won't trust you, and without trust, you can't lead effectively. You might have all the skills and knowledge in the world, but if your team can't rely on you to do the right thing, those attributes won't matter.

Leading with integrity is also about creating a culture where people feel empowered to speak up and act ethically, making the tough decisions and being willing to face the consequences, knowing that in the end, you'll be able to look in the mirror and be proud of what you see.

The choices we made during the pandemic at my company, were about who we are as a company, not just how we do business. Our choices set a precedent for how we handle adversity and showed our team and clients that we're willing to stand by our values, no matter what. That's the legacy I want to leave as a leader: one of integrity, trust, and unwavering commitment to doing what's right.

Integrity is as much about the culture you build and the example you set as it is about you. Creating an organization where everyone feels responsible for responding ethically and doing the right thing. The priority is leadership that not only inspires people but also stands the test of time.

Consistency: The Fourth Cornerstone of Authentic Leadership

Consistency forms the cornerstone on which teams and organizations build trust and credibility. Align your actions with your words and ensure that your behavior consistently reflects your values and commitments. This consistency sets a clear standard for everyone around you and creates a stable environment where people know what to expect.

Imagine the impact of a leader whose actions match their words. This kind of consistency isn't only about being dependable—it's about building trust that goes beyond compliance. It creates an atmosphere where people want to follow, not because they must, but because they believe in their leader's integrity and vision over time.

Additionally, consistency plays a crucial role in setting expectations. When your decision-making and problem-solving approaches are steady and clear, there is less confusion and ambiguity. Clarity allows your team to focus on their responsibilities with confidence, knowing they can rely on you to provide steady guidance, in challenging situations.

Consistency doesn't mean unwillingness to change. The most effective leaders stay true to their values and know their strategies must evolve as circumstances do. Their principles stay steady but how they apply them situationally adapts. This is what keeps organizations resilient and ready for whatever comes next.

I experienced the need for this balance firsthand during the pandemic when our organization, deemed "essential," was under pressure to continue operations despite the risks. Our projects typically required staff to travel and stay on-site for extended periods which felt increasingly unsafe as the pandemic escalated. While we wanted to meet our commitments to clients, we knew that prioritizing the well-being of our team was non-negotiable.

We respected everyone's safety concerns and comfort levels and made travel voluntary. This decision wasn't easy and likely cost us significant business as some clients pushed hard for us to resume full operations. But our commitment to our values was clear: no contract was worth compromising our team's safety. This choice reinforced our team's trust by showing them we were consistent in our commitment to their well-being, in spite of costly challenges. It was a real-world reminder that we can adapt our strategies without compromising our core values.

Being consistent means staying true to your core values while also being open to change when necessary. Maintain a clear direction but be willing to adjust your course as new information and challenges arise. This adaptability allows authentic leaders to navigate uncertainty with confidence and grace, ensuring their teams feel supported and guided through any situation.

Balancing consistency with flexibility can feel like walking a tightrope, but there are strategies that can help:

1. **Clear Communication:** Be transparent about why changes are happening and how they align with the organization's values and goals. This helps maintain trust when shifts in strategy are necessary.

2. **Root Decisions in Core Values:** Ensure you deeply connect all decisions, especially those representing a change in direction, to your core values. This approach maintains a thread of consistency amid change.

3. **Reflect Regularly:** Take time to reflect on your leadership practices to ensure they remain aligned with your stated values. This self-reflection allows you to course correct as needed and stay true to your authentic leadership style.

4. **Foster a Culture of Flexibility:** Encourage your team to view change as an evolution toward your shared mission and vision, not as a break from consistency. Show them that adapting is part of the journey, not a deviation from it.

Consistency requires self-reflection and continuous improvement. Ask yourself if your actions truly reflect your values or are there areas where you fall short. Consider how you show up as a leader. Are you dependable, even when things get tough? If there are areas where you struggle, reflect on why that might be and what you can do to improve. Use self-reflection to understand why you struggle in these areas.

Consistency in authentic leadership is about being a dependable anchor for your team while remaining open to change and growth. By mastering this balance, you not only build trust and credibility, but you also guide your organization through the complexities of an ever-changing world with resilience and agility.

My Journey: The EAST Way.

Our local high school has a powerful philosophy that guides the athletic programs, known as "The EAST Way." **E**ffort, **A**ttitude, **S**elflessness, and **T**oughness are more than just words on a banner. These are the principles that shape the mindset and behavior of young athletes. These philosophies mirror the foundational principles of authentic leadership: Consistency, Transparency, Integrity, and Self-Awareness.

Effort = Consistency: In sports, putting in consistent effort is non-negotiable. You must show up every day, whether you're playing in a high-stakes game or a routine practice and give your best. Consistency in leadership works the same way. Align your actions with your words, day in and day out, no matter the circumstances. Just as athletes build trust with their coaches and teammates by being reliable and hardworking, leaders build trust with their teams by being consistent in their values and behavior. Effort is the engine that drives consistency and allows leaders to be dependable, predictable, and trustworthy in the eyes of their teams.

Attitude = Transparency: A positive attitude on the field or court can shift the momentum of a game. Approach every situation with optimism and openness, even when things aren't going well. In leadership, this translates to transparency. An authentic leader's attitude sets the tone for the entire team. When leaders communicate openly, sharing both the good and the bad, they foster a culture of trust and honesty. You don't have to be overly optimistic or sugar-coat difficult situations. Instead, be transparent with your intentions and create an environment where everyone feels safe to express their thoughts and concerns. A leader's attitude towards openness can make all the difference in how connected and engaged a team feels.

Selflessness = Integrity: Selflessness in sports is about sacrificing personal glory for the good of the team. Whether it's making a pass instead of taking a shot or cheering on a teammate from the bench, a selfless player understands that the team's success is more important than individual accolades. This directly reflects integrity in leadership. Leaders with integrity put the needs of the organization and their people above their own. They make decisions that reflect the team's best interests, even when it means taking a more challenging path or turning down personal gain. Just as selfless athletes inspire their teammates, leaders who act with integrity inspire loyalty and commitment in their teams.

Toughness = Self-Awareness: In sports, toughness is physical strength and having the mental resilience to bounce back from setbacks and keep going. This kind of toughness requires a deep level of self-awareness that requires knowing your own strengths and limitations and understanding when to push forward and when to regroup. In leadership, self-awareness is the cornerstone of true resilience and allows leaders to recognize when they're pushing too hard or not enough. Be honest about limitations and seek support when needed. Being tough is about being attuned to yourself and your team. Know when to pivot and when to persevere.

The EAST Way builds strong athletes who are powerful leaders. By teaching young people to value effort, maintain a positive attitude, put others first, and be resilient in the face of adversity, the EAST Way lays the groundwork for authentic leadership. These are the same principles that guide prominent leaders in business and life. As you reflect on your own leadership journey, think about how you can apply the EAST Way in your day-to-day actions. Is your effort consistent? Are you maintaining a positive and transparent attitude? Are you acting with integrity, and are you tough enough to be self-aware? By embracing these values, you not only lead with authenticity, but set a powerful example for others to follow.

Many of the coaches and administrators at East High School not only teach "The EAST Way" but embody it through their own actions, demonstrating authentic leadership in every interaction. Their commitment to these principles is clear in the way they mentor and inspire young athletes to strive for excellence both on and off the field. I would be remiss if I didn't take this opportunity to express my gratitude to one coach in particular—the varsity boys' basketball coach at East. His unwavering support and encouragement have been invaluable to me throughout the process of drafting this book. Thank you, Coach Adkins, for your guidance, your dedication to our community, and for exemplifying what it means to lead with integrity and heart. Your impact extends far beyond the court, and I am deeply appreciative.

Final Thoughts: The Impact of Authentic Leadership

Authentic leadership means knowing your core beliefs and using that knowledge to lead with your complete self. By practicing the four cornerstones of authentic leadership, you create an environment where others feel safe enough to do the same, which in turn, creates a positive impact on your team, organization, and on the world around you.

As you move forward on your leadership journey, remember that authenticity is your greatest asset. It's what sets you apart and what will ultimately allow you to make the most meaningful contributions. Embrace your true self, lead with integrity and purpose, and inspire others to do the same.

Leadership is about being real, not being perfect. The essence of authentic leadership is showing up wholeheartedly, being open to learning and growth, and leading in a way that is true to who you are.

More than a technique or strategy, authentic leadership is a way of being. Lead from your authentic self, embrace your unique identity, and guide others with integrity, transparency, and genuine care. The journey to authenticity is both personal and ongoing, filled with opportunities for growth, connection, and profound impact.

Defining authenticity is merely the starting point. Whether you're a recent graduate stepping into your first leadership role or a seasoned professional navigating many new challenges, the genuine work of leadership begins when you align your actions with your core values. Leadership is an ongoing journey of growth, reflection, and self-discovery. In the next chapter, we'll dive into how you can start or refine your personal leadership journey and explore practical ways to connect who you are with how you lead. This is where your authentic leadership style truly takes shape.

2

The Authentic Leader's Journey

Embarking on the path of authentic leadership is akin to embarking on a voyage of self-discovery and purpose. Delve into the depths of your values, motivations, and aspirations and use that knowledge to shape your leadership style.

Becoming an authentic leader is a lifelong commitment to being true to yourself and your principles while guiding others with clarity and purpose. Each decision, interaction, and moment of reflection propels you towards authentic leadership aligned with your true self. Use this chapter as your guide to uncover your core values and develop a leadership vision that reflects your essence. Think of it as aligning your internal compass with the guiding light of your personal integrity and objectives.

The Power of First Impressions: A Hollywood Anecdote

Think back to your favorite movie or TV show. Who is that one memorable character that you can't seem to forget? Why did the actor who portrayed that character make a lasting impact on you? First impressions are powerful, and they don't just matter in Hollywood. They're just as crucial when starting your career.

For the sake of showing my age and my sense of humor, my two most memorable actors are classic examples of guys I still can't see differently today than when I saw them in first big roles. When I think of Steve Carell, I immediately picture him as Michael Scott from *The Office*. Before he was a household name, Steve Carell was relatively unknown. He had a few roles here and there, like his stint on *The Daily Show*, but it wasn't until he became the bumbling, loveable, and often cringe-worthy manager of Dunder Mifflin that he truly made his mark. Despite his later successes in films like *The Big Short* and *40-Year-Old Virgin*, many people will always see him as Michael Scott. That first impression was too strong.

Then there's Jeff Daniels, who might be a surprising example. He's had a long, impressive career, but let's be honest—most people from my generation probably think of him as Harry Dunne from *Dumb and Dumber*. That's a pretty stark contrast from his role as the serious, no-nonsense news anchor Will McAvoy in HBO's *The Newsroom*, right? When Will McAvoy makes the statement, "America is not the best country in the World," I respond with, "Harry, your hands are freezing." No matter how many awards you win or how diverse your roles are, often people will remember you for that one unforgettable first impression.

It's important to think about the impression you will make as you step into your first jobs. In the early days, figuring things out and finding your path can be overwhelming. My wife and I loved our 20s. We made lots of friends, emptied our bank account more than once on things we didn't need and, in general, did all the things you do in your 20s. I knew that no matter what I was doing in my personal life, being punctual, working long hours to learn my position, and listening were keys to building a strong first impression as a reliable and dedicated employee. The early impression you create in your career may have a lasting impact. Make those first impressions good. Be genuine and show others your true self. Allow your moral and ethical compass to guide you. Build your career diligently while embracing your youth as a young professional.

When meeting new colleagues, managers, or clients, be your authentic self. Show enthusiasm, willingness to learn, and ability to contribute. Be real. People will remember these qualities long after you've moved on in your career. Not unlike Carell's heartfelt portrayal of Michael Scott or Daniels' comedic genius as Harry Dunne made them memorable, your first impression in your professional life will be long lasting.

Embrace Self-Discovery: Exploring Personal Values and Motivations

Self-discovery is where authentic leadership begins. Knowing yourself by truly understanding what drives you, what you value, and what you stand for is crucial for everyone not just aspiring leaders. Your core values shape your decisions and behaviors, influencing how you interact with others and respond to challenges.

Consider for a moment what truly matters to you. Is it integrity, creativity, or perhaps empowering others? These values serve as your guideposts, shaping your actions and decisions. They're the principles you live by and the ones you're willing to stand up for, even when it's difficult. By acknowledging and adopting these values, you can lead authentically, purposefully, and in alignment with your true self.

I have always placed a high value on transparency and open communication. Early in my career, I led a high-profile project that encountered significant challenges. With a status meeting with senior leadership coming up, the pressure from local management to downplay these issues and present a more positive outlook to senior leadership was intense. Local management believed we could conceal the issues for one more month as we focused on realigning the project. Rightfully so, they were concerned about the status meeting spiraling into nothing more than a blaming session. While acknowledging the importance of accountability, I thought I could steer clear of blaming others in the meeting by emphasizing the need to concentrate on realigning the project instead of dwelling on past mistakes.

Instead of hiding the true state of the project, I was honest about the challenges we were facing. I admitted to past failures and announced that a root cause analysis would take place at a later date. I emphasized the steps being taken to tackle these issues and shifted the room's focus to the present rather than the past. Taking control of a room filled with leadership and management was not a simple decision, but I believed that being transparent and focusing our energy on what was most needed aligned with my core values of integrity, transparency, and courage. It was also what the team needed the most. Instead of dwelling on how we got to the point we were at, we needed to shift our focus towards finding solutions.

Fortunately, this approach worked. Senior leadership engaged and began removing barriers and approving our team's plan. Because of this approach, I gained the trust and respect of my team, local management, and senior leadership.

Tools for Self-Discovery

Finding out who you really are isn't something that happens overnight. It's more like piecing together a puzzle and each piece reveals a bit more about what makes you tick. Here are some practical tools that can help you on this journey:

Values Clarification Exercise: Make a list of your top 10 values. Then, choose your top five from that list. Ask yourself why each value is important to you. Reflect on how these values manifest in your life and work. This exercise can help you identify the values that truly shape your leadership style.

Reflective Journaling: Spend a few minutes each day or week writing your thoughts and experiences. What went well? What didn't? How did your actions and reactions reflect your core values? Over time, patterns will emerge that can provide deep insights into your motivations and behaviors.

Mindfulness and Meditation: These practices help quiet the external noise and bring attention to your inner thoughts and feelings. Taking just a few minutes each day to focus on your breathing and observe your thoughts without judgment can lead to profound realizations about what truly matters to you.

Feedback from others: Don't underestimate the value of outside perspectives. Ask trusted colleagues, mentors, or even friends for feedback on how they perceive your strengths and areas for growth. This crucial step in understanding how others perceive your strengths and weaknesses is difficult but necessary.

Personality and Leadership Assessments: Tools like the Myers-Briggs Type Indicator (MBTI), Clifton Strengths, or Emotional Intelligence (EQ) assessments can offer structured insights into your natural tendencies, helping you understand how they influence your leadership style and interactions. However, also be mindful of these assessment results and take them with a grain of salt.

After practicing the aforementioned strategies, I've developed my own list of top five core values in business and in life:

Teamwork: Team first. Hierarchy second.

- Prioritize collaboration over hierarchy empowers teams to share ideas and take ownership.
- Leadership isn't about titles—it's about creating a culture where everyone feels valued and included.
- When the team succeeds, the organization succeeds. Building unity starts with removing barriers.

Integrity: Make decisions that help myself and others sleep well at night

- Decisions grounded in thoughtfulness bring peace of mind to everyone involved.
- It's not just about short-term gains but ensuring actions align with long-term values and goals.
- When faced with tough choices, I ponder, "Can I sleep well tonight knowing I made this choice?"

Empathy: Understand and share the feelings and experiences of others.

- Don't be judgmental. You can never fully comprehend the difficulties that someone might be dealing with.
- Everyone has unseen challenges—approach others with empathy and an open mind.
- Compassion goes a long way. Instead of assuming, take time to listen and understand.

Being empathetic creates a culture where people feel safe to be themselves.

Equality: Don't hold other people to the expectations you hold for yourself.

- Everyone has unique strengths, challenges, and priorities—respecting that individuality builds trust.
- Setting realistic expectations for others helps avoid frustration and fosters collaboration.
- Lead by example without imposing personal standards on those around you.

Act with Fairness and Consistency: The Golden Rule for Adults

- Fairness means consistency in decisions and actions, while equity ensures everyone has access to opportunities.
- Treating vendors and clients fairly fosters trust and long-term partnerships, ensuring mutual respect and ethical practices.

Building trust starts with ensuring everyone—whether team members, clients, or vendors—feels seen, heard, and respected.

While these five values represent how I strive to live and lead, things like authenticity, transparency, consistency, self-awareness, and courage are also part of my core values, and I work to incorporate them in everything I do.

Overcoming Challenges in Self-Discovery

Self-discovery isn't always easy. You might uncover aspects that are uncomfortable or even surprising. It's normal to face resistance both from within, as you confront internal doubts and insecurities, and from external sources, like societal expectations or workplace culture. These challenges are essential steppingstones on the path to authentic leadership.

I once worked with a leader who was incredibly talented but struggled with perfectionism. She was so focused on avoiding mistakes that she rarely took risks, which stifled her team's creativity. Through coaching and self-reflection, she realized her fear of failure stemmed from a desire to prove herself. This realization allowed her to shift her mindset and embrace a more open experimental approach that ultimately transformed her team's dynamic and productivity. Today, she continues to be a highly regarded leader of teams that take on big ideas in our industry.

Overcoming these challenges requires resilience and a genuine self-assessment. By recognizing your strengths and limitations and accepting them as part of your unique leadership style, you can develop as a leader and create space for others to be authentic and transparent as well.

Set an Authentic Leadership Vision: Aligning Personal and Professional Goals

Creating your leadership vision is about dreaming big and figuring out how your personal values and professional goals align. You don't have to craft the perfect mission statement or plan every step of your career. Your vision is your compass and should reflect what truly matters to you.

Ask yourself: What kind of leader do I want to be? What reputation do I aim to establish? Your vision reflects your identity and values, not just your goals. Lead in a way that feels right for you, so your actions match your words, and your vision inspire others to get on board.

Road-map to Create Your Leadership Vision

Identify Your Core Values: Start by listing the five value statements that are most important to you. Think about how values like honesty, innovation, compassion, and perseverance have influenced your decisions and leadership style. Then, frame statements around the values you hold in the highest regards.

Define Your Leadership Purpose: Ask yourself, "What do I want to be known for as a leader? How do I influence those around me?" Your answers will shape your leadership vision.

Craft a Vision Statement: Using your values and purpose as a guide, write a brief statement that encapsulates your vision as a leader. For example, "I strive to lead with integrity and empathy, inspiring others to achieve their full potential while fostering a culture of collaboration and innovation."

Align Actions with Vision: For each value, list specific actions you can take to show that attribute every day in your leadership. For example, if "transparency" is a value, commit to sharing your decision-making process openly with your team.

Share Your Vision: Communicate your vision with your team in an authentic and personal way. Remember, you're sharing your passion and what you believe in, not delivering a rehearsed speech. When your team understands and believes in your vision, you create a shared sense of purpose and direction.

Inspiring Others with Your Vision

A leadership vision is powerful because it's personal. When you communicate your vision clearly and passionately, people pick up on that energy. They want to be part of something bigger than themselves. It's not only about your words; it's also about what you do. Living your vision—showing up consistently and authentically—is what builds trust and inspires others to follow.

I remember a time when I was leading a project that was struggling to gain traction. Despite everyone putting in the hours, frustration and disconnect lingered. I realized I hadn't been clear about why the project mattered and how it fit into the bigger picture. I stepped back, reconnected with the team, and shared my vision in a more personal manner. I talked about my excitement and why I believed in what we were doing. It wasn't a grand speech—just an honest conversation. The impact was immediate. They witnessed the connection of their work to a larger purpose, and that energy quickly spread.

The Ongoing Journey of Authentic Leadership

Authentic leadership is a continuous process of learning, adapting, and growing, not just as a leader, but as a person. Authentic leadership requires evolving with every experience, challenge, and interaction and using each as an opportunity to deepen your understanding of yourself and your impact on others. Embrace the idea that your leadership identity can evolve positively with time.

This journey requires a commitment to lifelong learning and a willingness to explore new perspectives, challenge your own assumptions, and seek experiences that push you beyond your comfort zone. There will be times when you make mistakes, face setbacks, and encounter situations that make you question your approach. However, these moments provide the most valuable lessons.

Think of the path to authentic leadership as a winding road rather than a straight line. Every turn, every obstacle, is an opportunity to refine your leadership style and deepen your self-awareness. Early in my career, I received an offer to lead a project far outside my area of expertise. Feeling unprepared and unsure of my abilities, my initial reaction was to turn it down. I embraced the challenge in order to push myself to grow. Experiences like these challenge us to rely on our teams, ask smarter questions, and embrace the learning process. These kinds of experiences shape who you are as a leader and help you build resilience and adaptability.

One of the most profound lessons I've learned is the importance of staying curious and humble. Becoming complacent or believing that you've "arrived" as a leader is easy, but authentic leadership is a journey without a finish line. It requires you to stay curious and always ask questions, explore new ideas, and be open to learning from anyone, regardless of their position or experience. To embrace humility, one must realize that there is always room for learning, no matter how much you already know.

Embrace Continuous Learning

Continuous learning is a hallmark of authentic leadership and is more than about attending workshops or reading books. You need to be open to learning in all forms—whether it's a new skill, a different cultural perspective, or insights from someone with a completely unique background. Here are some ways to expand your horizons:

Seek Diverse Experiences: Don't limit your learning to what's directly related to your role. Attend workshops on topics outside your usual focus, engage in volunteer work, or travel to places that challenge your worldview. These experiences provide fresh insights and new ways of thinking that you can incorporate in your leadership practice.

Learn from Your Team: Some of the best lessons come from unexpected places, like a junior team member who sees a problem from a unique angle. Once, an intern recommended a process alteration that initially appeared too daring. But after listening and reflecting, I realized her idea addressed a blind spot I hadn't considered. This experience reminded me to always stay open to learning, regardless of the source.

Read Broadly and Deeply: Books, articles, and even podcasts can be substantial sources of inspiration and knowledge. Don't just stick to leadership or business topics. Explore literature, history, psychology, and even fiction. These diverse perspectives can enrich your understanding of human nature and leadership.

Engage in Reflective Practice: Take time on a regular basis to reflect on your experiences. Consider what went well after completing a major project, tough decision, or difficult conversation. What could you have done differently? What did you learn about yourself in this process? This habit of reflection helps you internalize lessons and continuously refine your leadership approach.

Tie Personal Growth to Organizational Impact

As leaders grow in their authenticity, their personal evolution naturally extends into their professional spheres. The more grounded and self-aware you become, the more positively you can influence the surrounding culture. Your journey is about how your growth as an authentic leader can transform your team and organization alongside your own development.

Setting the tone for others is accomplished by leading with genuine understanding and purpose. People can sense when you're authentic, and this creates a ripple effect that reaches every corner of the organization. Authentic leaders inspire others to bring their full selves to work and foster an environment where trust, creativity, and collaboration thrive. The more leaders invest in their own growth, the more they unlock growth across their teams, the culture, and their organization's future.

Impact on Organizational Culture

Your personal journey has a profound ripple effect on your entire organization. Leading authentically sets the tone for the whole team and creates an environment where honesty, integrity, and genuine connection can flourish. People feel more comfortable being themselves, sharing ideas, and taking risks. A culture of authenticity boosts morale and leads to better business results.

In the earlier example, when I took on that challenging project, I realized how my personal growth influenced my leadership approach. As I became more comfortable with my own vulnerabilities and more open to learning, I noticed a shift in my team as well. They mirrored my willingness to ask questions, admit mistakes, and embrace new ideas. This openness fostered a culture of trust and collaboration that drove the project and our team to new heights.

Building a Culture of Trust and Openness

One of the most significant ways authentic leadership shapes organizational culture is by building real trust. Trust cannot be forced. It is earned through consistent, transparent, and empathetic leadership. When leaders are open about their own challenges and actively listen to their team members' concerns, they create a safe space where everyone feels empowered to speak up and contribute.

For example, during a difficult restructuring period at a previous organization, I was completely upfront about the changes we were facing and what it meant for each team member. This wasn't a straightforward conversation, and I knew it would create some anxiety. However, I also knew that trying to soften the truth or withholding information would only breed distrust. That honesty, though painful, allowed us to rebuild the team's morale and cohesion. Over time, that openness built a culture of resilience and mutual respect, proving that authenticity is about being real, even when it's hard.

Encouraging Innovation and Creativity

An authentic culture also encourages innovation and creativity. When people feel safe enough to express themselves without fear of judgment or retribution, they are more likely to take creative risks and propose bold ideas. In this setting, people embrace failure as a chance to learn, not as something to avoid at any cost.

Imagine a scenario where a team member proposes a radical alternative approach to a long-standing process. In a culture characterized by fear and inflexibility, team members could easily overlook or not speak up about this idea. In a culture of authenticity, we welcome, explore, and look to implement suggestions, resulting in breakthroughs that may not have happened otherwise.

One of my proudest moments came from encouraging this kind of environment. A junior employee suggested a major change to how we managed client communications. This suggestion, if implemented, would have required a complete overhaul of our current system. Rather than dismiss the idea because of its scale, we engaged in open discussions and evaluated the pros and cons together as a team. Eventually, we piloted the idea on a small scale, and it turned out to be an immense success. Not only did this idea improve efficiency but it also enhanced client satisfaction. We made this achievement possible by fostering a culture that values all voices and promotes innovation.

Similarly, a colleague of mine once shared a story about a tech startup where the CEO required employees to spend 20% of their time working on "passion projects"—ideas and innovations outside of their regular job scope. This initiative, inspired by the authentic leadership ethos of empowering others to explore their interests, led to the development of a new product line that became one of the company's top revenue generators. In an environment where people express their creativity and leaders truly value their contributions, this kind of innovation can thrive.

These examples illustrate that when you create a culture where people feel safe and empowered to share their ideas, remarkable things can happen. The key is to support and encourage creative thinking, to celebrate both successes and learning from failures, and to trust in your team's potential to drive innovation and growth.

Creating a Sustainable and Inclusive Culture

Authentic leadership also contributes to building a sustainable and inclusive culture. Leaders who are genuine and transparent set a precedent for how everyone in the organization should interact with respect, honesty, and empathy. This helps create an inclusive environment that celebrates diversity of thought and background instead of suppressing it.

While having a diverse and inclusive workplace is a social benefit, it's also a strategic advantage. Studies have shown that organizations with diverse leadership teams are more innovative and perform better financially. But achieving true inclusion requires more than just hiring people from diverse backgrounds. To achieve true inclusion, organizations should cultivate a culture that fosters a sense of belonging for everyone. This culture should also value unique perspectives and enable individuals to be their authentic selves at work.

Authentic leaders are pivotal in fostering this environment. By openly discussing their own experiences and challenges, they invite others to do the same, breaking down barriers and building bridges of understanding and trust. Leaders committed to creating a thriving workplace build this culture through their daily actions and decisions.

Linking Personal Growth to Organizational Transformation

As your journey of personal growth unfolds, its impact on your organization becomes clearer. As an authentic leader, you create a thriving culture where individuals feel empowered to bring their best selves to work. When authenticity is at the core of your leadership, it resonates throughout the organization, fostering a culture of trust, innovation, and resilience.

Remember, the journey of authentic leadership is ongoing and is filled with opportunities for growth, connection, and positive change. As you continue to develop and refine your leadership approach, your organization will reflect that growth, becoming a place where people contribute with inspiration, collaborate, and excel.

Authentic leaders don't have all the answers and don't follow a set of prescribed behaviors. Bring your true self into your role every day and lead in a way that resonates with who you genuinely are. This complex and ongoing journey is filled with moments of self-discovery, vulnerability, and growth. It's about understanding your own values and motivations and then using that understanding to guide your actions and decisions. As you've explored in this chapter, the path to authentic leadership is deeply personal, but also profoundly impactful on those around you.

Again, a key challenge in authentic leadership is the readiness to embrace vulnerability. There's often a misconception that leaders need to be invincible and project unwavering strength and certainty. But true leadership is about embracing your humanity and being willing to admit when you don't have all the answers. Show your team that it's okay to be unsure, to make mistakes, and to grow from them. Instead of undermining your authority, this kind of openness builds trust and connection by allowing your team to see you as a real, relatable person rather than a distant figurehead.

Consider your own leadership journey. Have you experienced pressure to meet others' expectations or fit into a specific leadership mold? Maybe you've struggled with balancing your personal values with the demands of your role or felt uncertain about how much of your true self to reveal. These challenges are a natural part of the process. Authentic leadership is about navigating these complexities with honesty and courage, trusting that your genuine self is the most powerful tool you have.

Lead with Authenticity in Every Moment

Authentic leadership is seen in every interaction, conversation, and choice you make, including big actions and important decisions. It is about how you listen, respond, and support your team, especially in tough times. Make sure your words and actions match up. This consistency builds trust and encourages others to be authentic, too.

Think back to the stories and examples we've explored in this chapter about leaders who took risks by being open about their struggles, who encouraged creativity by fostering a safe environment, and who navigated tough situations with transparency and integrity. These acts of leadership interconnect. They are reflections of a deeper commitment to authenticity that permeates everything these leaders do. The leaders in these examples didn't just talk about their values, they lived them. In doing so, they inspired those around them to do the same.

The Ripple Effect of Authentic Leadership

The impact of authentic leadership extends far beyond the individual leader and into the entire organizational culture. Authentic leaders create a workplace where people feel valued, engaged, and empowered to contribute their best. When leaders are authentic, others follow. Authenticity creates a ripple effect that touches every aspect of the organization from team dynamics and innovation to employee satisfaction and performance. For example, a leader being open about their own challenges encourages team members to be more honest about their own obstacles, which encourages transparency, and leads to faster problem-solving and deeper trust.

Reflect on how your own journey towards authentic leadership has influenced those around you. Have you noticed changes in your team's behavior or the overall atmosphere in your workplace? Perhaps you've seen an increase in collaboration, creativity, or openness as your team feels more comfortable bringing their full selves to work. These shifts, while sometimes subtle, are powerful indicators of the positive impact authentic leadership can have.

Overcoming the Challenges of Authentic Leadership

The path to authentic leadership is not without its challenges. Expect moments of resistance, whether it comes from within or from others. You may doubt your ability to lead authentically or fear that revealing too much of your true self will make you vulnerable. While these fears are understandable, they underscore the importance of authenticity.

Embracing authenticity means being willing to take those risks. It means standing by your values, even when it's difficult, and being open about your journey, even when it's uncomfortable. You'll find strength in vulnerability and use it to build deeper connections with those around you. Show up fully, with all your strengths and imperfections, and lead from a place of genuine integrity and purpose. Remember, authenticity is about being real, not being perfect.

Your Leadership Legacy

As you continue on your journey of authentic leadership, consider the legacy you want to leave behind. What is the lasting impression you want your leadership to leave on people? How do you plan to shape both your organization's culture and the lives of those under your leadership? Authentic leadership is about the impact you have today and creating a lasting legacy of trust, empowerment, and positive change.

Consider the leaders who have motivated you. Chances are, they weren't perfect. Perhaps they had their quirks and made mistakes, but their genuineness made them unforgettable. They led with their hearts as much as their heads, and they weren't afraid to let their teams see who they really were. Their flaws showed that being an outstanding leader is about being real, relatable, and committed to making a meaningful impact.

Embrace the Journey Ahead

As you move forward in your leadership journey, remember that authenticity is your greatest strength. It's what makes your leadership unique and what will ultimately help you make the most meaningful impact. Don't be afraid to share your vision, your struggles, and your excitement. Let your team see the person behind the title. When you lead with authenticity, you're not just guiding a team—you're building trust, fostering connection, and creating a culture where everyone feels empowered to be their best selves.

So, take a deep breath, embrace the journey, and remember: the world needs more authentic leaders and fewer perfectionists. Keep being you and striving to lead with authenticity and purpose. Your unique voice, vision, and values are exactly what your team and your organization need.

3

Cultivating Trust and Transparency

In the intricate dance of leadership, trust and transparency are the music that sets the rhythm for relationships within any organization. Without them, even the best-intentioned leaders struggle to connect with their teams. In this chapter, we'll explore the art of building trust through open communication and how to strike the right balance between honesty and privacy that defines transparent leadership, which cultivates an environment where team members feel valued, heard, and respected, and fosters a culture of openness that drives success for everyone involved.

True leadership requires more than just good ideas and vision. It demands that leaders attempt to engage in honest conversations, be open about their intentions, and remain steadfast when dealing with tough decisions. Building trust and being transparent are ongoing practices that grow and develop as you and your organization face new challenges. This chapter doesn't just cover *what* of trust and transparency. We will also dive deep into the *how* behind creating an atmosphere that promotes true openness and connection.

I'll share real-life examples, tools, and strategies that will help you understand the nuances of fostering trust while still respecting boundaries and how transparency can lead to an authentic and productive team culture. Let's dive into why these principles matter, how they can transform the workplace, and the steps you can take to strengthen your leadership approach.

Establishing Trust

Trust is essential for effective leadership and the glue that binds teams together. Leaders must build trust over time through consistent, authentic actions. Trust is not something to be demanded. A study by Leroy, Palanski, and Simons examines how authentic leadership influences employee behaviors through two critical mediating factors: identification and trust. (Leroy et al., 2012) Their research underscores that authentic leaders enhance team dynamics and create a strong sense of connection between employees and the organization. By aligning their actions with the organization's values, leaders foster identification, which strengthens emotional bonds and lays the groundwork for innovative behaviors. For example, when leaders model transparency and integrity, employees are more likely to reflect these traits in their roles, resulting in heightened engagement and productivity. Trust, as highlighted in the study, plays a pivotal role by acting as a buffer against the fear of failure and empowering employees to approach challenges confidently and with creativity. This combination of identification and trust exemplifies how authentic leadership can inspire a thriving organizational culture. Open communication, a conduit that fosters connection, understanding, and mutual respect, is at the heart of this trust-building process.

Open communication involves much more than just sharing information. It's about creating a two-way dialogue where team members feel heard, valued, and respected and an environment where everyone feels safe to express their ideas, concerns, and aspirations without fear of judgment or repercussions. When leaders prioritize open communication, they reinforce their trustworthiness by showing that every voice matters.

Think about a time when you felt heard at work. Being heard made you feel valued and motivated to contribute even more. That's the power of genuine communication. When leaders listen and communicate openly, they create an atmosphere of psychological safety, a critical ingredient for high-performing teams. Team members feel more connected, more engaged, and more willing to bring their authentic selves to the table when they feel safe enough to do so.

Building trust is a process that requires ongoing effort. Every interaction is an opportunity to either strengthen or weaken the trust within a team. A leader who is able to communicate openly and fosters transparency stands out. Let's explore some practical strategies for enhancing open communication that can help build trust within your team.

Strategies for Enhancing Open Communication

Active Listening: One of the simplest yet most powerful ways to build trust is through active listening. This means giving your full attention to the speaker and focusing on what he or she is saying rather than planning your response or getting distracted. Active listening involves hearing and understanding the perspectives of team members, validating their contributions, and addressing their concerns thoughtfully. By practicing active listening, leaders communicate the value of team members' voices and input. Small things like maintaining eye contact, nodding, and asking follow-up questions make a big difference in how heard someone feels.

Regular Feedback: Trust thrives in an environment where feedback is both given and received transparently. Instituting a culture of continuous feedback helps ensure everyone agrees and that there are no hidden surprises. Constructive feedback, delivered with empathy and respect, shows the leader's investment in their team members' growth. It's not just about pointing out areas for improvement—it's also about celebrating achievements and recognizing progress. Leaders acknowledging accomplishments reinforces a culture of appreciation and motivation. On the flip side, team members feeling safe enough to offer feedback to their leaders fosters a sense of equality and shared responsibility for the team's success.

Transparency in decision-making: Leaders should involve their team members in the decision-making process to build trust and engagement. Leaders should explain their decisions, their reasoning, and how these decisions support organizational goals. This approach helps team members feel a sense of ownership and understand the bigger picture. Even when the news is not positive, being transparent about challenges shows honesty and courage, which are crucial for building trust.

Create Safe Spaces for Dialogue: Another important aspect of open communication is creating safe spaces for dialogue. Leaders should encourage team members to voice their thoughts, whether in formal meetings or casual conversations. This might mean setting aside dedicated time in team meetings for open discussion or establishing channels where people can share ideas or concerns without fear of backlash. Knowing they have a platform for open communication assures team members that their contributions and well-being matter to the organization.

Consistency and Follow-Through: We build trust through consistency and doing what we say we will do. Leaders who follow through on their commitments, no matter how small, demonstrate reliability. Avoid making promises you can't keep. Instead, be honest about what's possible and be transparent when things change. Consistency between words and actions reassures team members they can count on their leader, even when times get tough.

We build trust by consistently showing up, actively listening, being transparent, and ensuring everyone's voice is heard. When trust is the present and unwavering, teams are more resilient, more innovative, and more connected. By fostering open communication, leaders lay the groundwork for a culture where trust can thrive, enabling the entire organization to flourish.

The Art of Being Transparent: Balancing Honesty and Privacy

Transparency in leadership is about honesty and openness in actions, decisions, and communications. It's not just about sharing information, but doing so with clarity and intent, ensuring that team members understand the context and rationale behind leadership decisions. This level of openness fosters a sense of inclusion and respect, reinforcing the trust that is foundational to effective leadership.

However, transparency is not without its challenges. It requires discernment to strike a balance between the need for openness and confidentiality in certain situations. This balance is crucial in maintaining trust, as indiscriminate sharing can be as damaging as unwarranted secrecy. Leaders must learn to navigate these nuances to ensure that transparency is both meaningful and responsible.

Navigating the Balance between Honesty and Privacy

Balancing honesty and privacy is one of the trickiest aspects of authentic leadership. Leaders need to determine when and what information to share while respecting privacy and confidentiality. Navigating this balance requires thoughtful consideration and clear communication.

Understand the Boundaries: Transparency is important. Knowing what and when to share is crucial. Some information, such as personal employee details, strategic plans, or legal matters, must remain private. Understanding these boundaries is key to building trust. When leaders are clear about what they can disclose, they show respect for the organization and its people.

Clear Communication Policies: Establishing clear communication policies helps create a consistent approach to transparency. These guidelines should detail the information to be shared, its dissemination method, and the channels available to team members for clarification or further information. A structured approach to communication enables leaders to ensure everyone receives appropriate information and knows where to seek clarification. This clarity helps prevent misunderstandings and fosters a culture where information flows freely.

Considerations: Ethical standards must always align with transparency. The drive for openness should never compromise the privacy rights of individuals or the ethical integrity of the organization. Leaders need to consider the potential impact of sharing certain information and weigh it against the need for confidentiality. For example, while honesty about the organization's challenges is important, leaders should avoid disclosing details that could jeopardize team security or breach of trust. Leaders who navigate these ethical considerations thoughtfully set a powerful example for their teams.

The Balancing Act: Honesty vs. Privacy

Transparency is not always black and white. Sometimes honesty and privacy seem at odds, requiring careful navigation. Below are some real-world scenarios where leaders must walk the line between openness and discretion. From handling sensitive personal information to navigating organizational challenges, these examples highlight how important balancing honesty with the respect for privacy that every individual deserves is.

---

1. **Performance Reviews:** Sharing feedback with an employee is essential, but respecting their privacy by not discussing their performance with others is equally important.

---

2. **Team Conflict:** Addressing conflicts between team members requires honesty about issues while keeping the details private to avoid unnecessary tension among others, especially if they are not involved in the conflict.

---

3. **Financial Challenges:** Being open about company financial difficulties can build trust, but leaders must be cautious not to divulge sensitive information that could cause panic or harm employee morale.

---

4. **Promotions and Raises:** Communication about promotion processes is important, but specific reasons behind individual decisions should remain private to maintain respect for all candidates.

---

5. **Health Concerns:** If an employee is facing health challenges, acknowledging their absence is necessary, but sharing personal health details with the rest of the team is a breach of privacy.

---

6. **Strategic Changes:** Leaders need to share the reasons behind strategic changes to align the team, but sensitive details such as pending mergers should remain confidential until confirmed legally.

---

7. **Project Failures:** Sharing lessons learned from a project failure is beneficial, but avoiding placing blame on specific individuals keeps the conversation constructive and respectful.

---

8. **Salary Transparency:** Providing general guidelines about compensation can promote fairness, but disclosing individual salaries can create discord and is inappropriate, except in unique situations.

---

9. **Legal Matters:** Acknowledging when legal issues affect the organization is important. However, to protect the company, we must maintain the confidentiality of details regarding ongoing litigation.

---

10. **Succession Planning:** Discussing leadership development fosters growth, but individual succession plans should be private to avoid creating competitive or anxious environments.

---

11. **Employee Termination:** Explaining that a team member is no longer with the company is necessary, but sharing personal details behind the termination violates privacy.

---

12. **Personal Mistakes:** While leaders admitting their own mistakes models vulnerability, they must be mindful not to over-share details that could harm their credibility or relationships.

Balancing honesty and privacy requires you, as a leader, to be intentional in your communication. You have to be open while also being mindful of the implications of that openness. Effective leaders understand that authentic transparency is not about disclosing everything but about sharing what is relevant and necessary to foster trust, support team engagement, and drive collective success. As highlighted by Leroy, Palanski, and Simons, when leaders align their communication with organizational values, they foster a sense of identification among team members.

This identification strengthens trust, making navigating uncertainty with confidence easier for employees. By embodying transparency and aligning it with ethical considerations, leaders reinforce trust, making team members feel respected, and in turn, enable the organization to thrive.

Driving Engagement, Productivity, and Team Morale

More than ever, people want to know who they're following and why. According to the Edelman Trust Barometer (ETB), a respected annual study spanning over 30 countries, businesses are now the most trusted global institution, with 62% of respondents expressing confidence in organizations led by ethical and transparent leaders. This finding's abstract endorsement of trust also shows tangible implications for engagement, productivity, and team morale. (*Edelman Trust Barometer*, 2023.)

For example, the ETB 2023 report revealed that employees are 76% more likely to remain loyal to organizations where leadership shows openness and alignment with stated values. Transparency in decision-making plays a pivotal role in this loyalty. Employees want to understand the *why* behind leadership choices, whether it's a strategic shift, an organizational restructuring, or even day-to-day decisions that impact team priorities. Without this context, teams may feel disconnected or undervalued, resulting in disengagement and diminished performance.

Transparency is crucial during periods of uncertainty. In recent years, the ETB has consistently shown that employees value frequent and honest communication from leaders, especially during times of crisis or change.

This expectation reflects a fundamental human need to feel included and informed. When leaders rise to meet this need by discussing challenges, addressing employee concerns, and sharing updates on progress, they foster not only trust but also a shared sense of resilience.

The positive impact of trust and transparency extends beyond individual engagement. It strengthens team dynamics, enabling better collaboration, innovation, and problem-solving. Employees who trust their leaders are more likely to contribute ideas, take calculated risks, and support each other in achieving shared goals. As the ETB study highlights, leaders who communicate create an environment where employees feel not just valued but also empowered to thrive.

Attracting and Retaining Top Talent

In an era of valuing authenticity, leaders practicing openness and mutual respect differentiate themselves, attracting and keeping top talent. Workplaces that recognize contributions, listen to employees, and have trustworthy leaders attract talented individuals.

A reputation for trust and transparency makes an organization more attractive to prospective employees. During the recruitment process, candidates often look for signs of the organization's culture and values. Leaders who show a commitment to these principles can attract high-caliber talent who share similar values. When potential employees see that a company prioritizes honest communication, ethical leadership, and a supportive environment, they are more likely to be drawn to the organization. Transparency about things like company goals, challenges, and expectations during the hiring process also help set the tone for an authentic and trusting relationship from the start.

Retention is important. Employees who feel trusted and valued are more likely to stay, grow, and contribute to the company's success over the long term. This stability benefits the organization by reducing turnover costs and keeping valuable institutional knowledge. When leaders communicate about career development opportunities and provide honest feedback, employees are more motivated to advance within the organization rather than seeking opportunities elsewhere. A culture of transparency also ensures that employees understand their career paths and feel supported in their growth, which strengthens their loyalty to the company.

Consider a company known for its transparent communication and ethical leadership. This reputation can become a powerful tool in attracting top talent that's looking for a workplace that aligns with their values. Once these individuals are part of the organization, the same principles of trust and transparency help to keep them, creating a virtuous cycle of attracting and keeping the best people. Leaders who are open about the company's direction and involve employees in shaping that direction create a sense of ownership and belonging. This not only enhances engagement but also makes employees feel they are an integral part of the organization's journey.

Trust and transparency contribute to a positive work environment where employees feel safe, respected, and empowered. When team members trust their leaders, they are more likely to voice their ideas, share their concerns, and contribute to innovation. This kind of culture is not only attractive to potential hires but also crucial for retaining existing talent. Employees want to work in an environment where they feel they can make an impact, and where their leaders commit to honesty and mutual respect.

Attracting and keeping top talent requires more than just competitive salaries or benefits. Potential employees want an environment where they feel valued, heard, and connected to a greater purpose. Trust and transparency build such an environment which attracts and inspires talented individuals to stay and grow. By adopting these values, leaders create a workplace that stands out and attracts top talent, nurtures their growth, and keeps them for the long haul.

Practical Steps for Cultivating Trust and Transparency

Cultivating trust and transparency is an ongoing practice that requires intentionality, consistency, and the ability to adapt. The ETB also reinforces the importance of transparency in leadership. The 2023 edition found that organizations where leaders communicate openly are more likely to keep loyal and engaged employees. This underscores the need for leaders to integrate trust-building practices into their everyday interactions with teams.

Open Forums and Town Hall Meetings

One of the most effective ways to foster transparency is by creating spaces where employees can ask questions and express concerns. Regular open forums or town hall meetings provide opportunities for direct dialogue between leadership and team members. Leaders should approach these sessions with candor and make sure the sessions are inclusive and welcoming.

By sharing organizational goals, addressing challenges, and responding to employee feedback in these forums, leaders reinforce a culture of trust and alignment:

Transparent Reporting: Transparent reporting practices are essential for building trust across teams. Sharing performance metrics, project updates, and the rationale behind key decisions demystifies leadership actions and helps employees feel more connected to the organization's mission. According to the ETB study, employees are more likely to trust leaders who explain the *why* behind their decisions. Doing so aligns communication with organizational values. Transparency in reporting can also foster a shared sense of purpose, as team members understand how their contributions align with broader goals.

Feedback Mechanisms: Establishing clear and accessible feedback mechanisms is another critical step. Leaders can introduce channels like anonymous surveys, suggestion boxes, or dedicated feedback sessions to ensure employees feel safe sharing their thoughts without fear of reprisal. The ETB emphasizes the importance of responsiveness. Leaders who listen to employee concerns and provide timely updates on actions taken are far more likely to cultivate trust. Feedback loops that encourage two-way communication signal to employees that their voices matter.

Recognition Programs: Recognition programs play a vital role in promoting trust and transparency by celebrating employees who exemplify these values. Leaders might introduce peer-nominated awards or public acknowledgments to reinforce the importance of transparency and mutual respect. These initiatives not only motivate employees but also set a powerful example of how to live out trust and transparency in our everyday actions.

Leadership Accountability: Leaders themselves must model the values they wish to see in their teams. This includes being open about their own challenges and learning experiences. The ETB study underscores that employees are more likely to trust leaders who show vulnerability and admit when they don't have all the answers. Such moments of honesty humanize leadership and strengthen the bond between leaders and their teams.

Consistency and Follow-Through: Consistency is key. Over time, repeated actions aligning with stated values builds trust. Leaders who follow through on promises, whether it's implementing a new policy or addressing specific concerns, demonstrate reliability and integrity. The ETB highlights employees feel a stronger sense of stability and confidence in leaders who maintain a consistent approach, even during times of uncertainty.

Transparency is about sharing the right information at the right time to foster trust, alignment, and engagement, without sharing every single detail. By adopting these practical steps, leaders cultivate an environment where trust and transparency drive organizational success.

The Future of Leadership: Embracing Trust and Transparency

As leadership expectations evolve, transparency and trust have become non-negotiable traits. The Edelman Trust Barometer continues to reveal that employees feel more engaged and motivated when leaders communicate openly and align their actions with their words. This reflects a broader shift toward valuing leadership that is not only effective but also ethical and human.

The increasing complexity of today's business environment which is shaped by factors like remote work, digital transformation, and corporate social responsibility, makes transparency a critical leadership skill. Remote work, for instance, has challenged traditional methods of communication and collaboration. In this context, leaders must find new ways to connect with their teams, ensuring that everyone remains informed and aligned. Transparency in remote settings might involve more frequent updates, virtual town halls, or tools that facilitate open communication.

Digital transformation also presents unique opportunities and challenges for transparency. On one hand, technology enables greater data sharing and communication, making it easier for leaders to keep their teams informed. However, the increased use of digital communication raises ethical questions about privacy and the use of data (Chamorro-Premuzic, T. & Buchband, R., 2020). The ETB study highlights the importance of addressing these concerns proactively. By explaining data collection, storage, and usage, transparent leaders build trust and show their dedication to ethical practices.

Corporate social responsibility (CSR) is another area where trust and transparency play a vital role. Consumers, employees, and investors increasingly expect organizations to show ethical behavior and a commitment to social and environmental issues. The ETB shows employees are more likely to trust and engage with companies that communicate openly about their CSR efforts. Transparency in the areas of sustainability goals, community impact, or diversity and inclusion initiatives, and other issues strengthens trust and builds organizational credibility.

The future of leadership lies in creating environments where people feel empowered, respected, and connected to a shared purpose. Trust and transparency allow these environments to thrive. Leaders who embrace these values will not only build stronger teams but also position their organizations for lasting success in an ever-changing world.

Final Thoughts: The Impact of Trust and Transparency

Cultivating trust and transparency within an organization has far-reaching implications. These principles not only enhance team cohesion and morale but also drive engagement and productivity. When employees trust their leaders and understand the vision behind decisions, they are more likely to commit to shared goals and contribute to the organization's success.

In a world that values authenticity, fostering an environment of openness and mutual respect differentiates effective leaders. Leroy, Palanski, and Simons highlight that authentic leadership, rooted in alignment with organizational values, deepens emotional connections and builds trust—foundations of resilient and innovative teams. Transparency enables organizations to weather challenges while priming them for growth and success.

Building trust and transparency is an ongoing journey requiring consistent attention and intention. It involves cultivating a culture where open communication thrives, honesty is balanced with respect for privacy, and every team member feels valued. This chapter has outlined pathways to foster such a culture, demonstrating the pivotal role of leadership in creating an environment where trust and transparency are not just ideals but lived realities.

Authentic leadership is about understanding and valuing the human element at the core of every organization. Leaders who prioritize trust and transparency empower their teams to operate with confidence, creativity, and purpose. As we navigate our leadership journeys, remember that the culture we cultivate today built on the unwavering pillars of trust, respect, and open communication. will shape the impact we have tomorrow.

4

Leading with Integrity

The Theranos Scandal: A Cautionary Tale of Integrity Lost

In the mid-2000s, Elizabeth Holmes, a young Stanford dropout, captivated Silicon Valley with her ambitious vision for Theranos, a healthcare company she claimed would revolutionize blood testing. A quirky but authentic Holmes attracted prominent investors and gained fame as a young entrepreneur. By the time she was 30, she had become the world's youngest self-made female billionaire, thanks to the promise of a technology that could run hundreds of diagnostic tests with just a few drops of blood.

However, behind this glossy exterior lay a strange reality. The company's flagship device, the Edison, could not reliably perform the tests it was supposed to. For years, Holmes and her executives misled investors, regulators, and patients while maintaining a facade of success. Employees who raised concerns were silenced. Theranos' leadership created a toxic culture full of fear and secrecy.

In 2015, *The Wall Street Journal* exposed these cracks. Investigative journalist John Carreyrou's reporting revealed widespread fraud, rigged tests, and data manipulation to hide the technology's failures (Carreyrou, 2018). By 2018, the company had collapsed, and authorities charged Holmes and her COO with multiple counts of fraud. A story of visionary leadership transformed into a cautionary tale illustrating the consequences of prioritizing ambition over integrity.

The rise and fall of Theranos is not just a story of technological failure. It's a stark reminder of the critical role integrity plays in leadership. Holmes' desire to disrupt an industry clouded her judgment and led to ethical compromises. Instead of admitting when things weren't working and pivoting with transparency, she doubled down on deception. While you have to have a vision and ambition to lead, you must also make ethical decisions, even when things go wrong. This case underscores the point that without integrity, even the most innovative ideas can collapse, and the repercussions can be devastating, not only for the leader but for everyone involved.

The Importance of Integrity in Leadership

At its core, leadership is about influence. Every action, word, and decision a leader makes sends ripples through their team, organization, and industry. This influence is a powerful tool that can shape outcomes, motivate individuals, and guide the entire company's direction. However, without integrity as a guiding principle, leadership can lose its ethical grounding. Integrity ensures responsible use of this influence for the greater good and not for personal gain or unethical purposes.

Integrity is non-negotiable in leadership because it separates leaders who care about the well-being of their teams and organizations from those who are concerned with appearances or short-term success. When leaders act without integrity, their influence becomes hollow and focused more on outward success than on doing what is right. This can lead to toxic work cultures, erosion of trust, and ultimately, the downfall of both the leader and the organization, as seen in the infamous case of Elizabeth Holmes and Theranos.

Integrity goes beyond avoiding unethical behavior. It requires a strong moral compass that aligns actions with core values. A leader with integrity is transparent when challenges arise, honest when things go wrong, and accountable for mistakes. These qualities are both trustworthy and exemplary. Leaders who uphold their values in times of difficulty foster a culture of openness and reliability where team members feel secure in expressing concerns and offering solutions.

However, individuals can use influence without integrity for the wrong reasons by steering decisions and actions that may benefit a few at the expense of others. Many influential leaders throughout history have used their power for self-serving or unethical purposes. This misuse of influence underscores the critical role that a moral compass plays in leadership. Being authentic and transparent is not enough. An authentic leader must also have a clear sense of right and wrong to guide their decisions. A leader's moral compass ensures that their authenticity does not stray into harmful or unethical territory.

For young professionals stepping into leadership roles, the pressure to succeed often feels overwhelming. Though the temptation to take shortcuts or compromise values for short-term success is real, these actions have long-term consequences. The true mark of great leadership is not the speed of someone's rise to the top, but their steadfast commitment to values. Integrity provides the foundation for long-term, sustainable success, both for the leader and their organization.

Leaders with integrity create environments of trust where teams thrive, and innovation flourishes. By aligning their influence with their values and moral compass, they ensure that their leadership leaves a positive impact, both inside and outside the organization. In the end, this combination of integrity and ethical influence is what distinguishes outstanding leaders from mediocre ones.

Building Trust Through Integrity

Trust and integrity are central to effective leadership. A leader's actions and decisions set the tone for the organization, influencing how employees engage with one another and with the broader mission. Studies affirm that integrity-driven leadership creates environments where employees feel valued and empowered.

A 2023 study in *Frontiers in Psychology* found that ethical leadership positively influences employees' ethical work behavior, with organizational commitment serving as a mediating factor (Guo et al., 2023). Leaders who act with transparency and fairness create workplaces where employees trust that their contributions matter. This trust translates into greater collaboration and productivity, as team members feel secure in their roles and confident in their leaders' intentions.

Day-to-day consistency in ethical behavior, not grand gestures, builds trust. A leader who aligns her actions with her values sends a coherent message that she is dependable and worthy of trust. This predictability fosters a culture of openness where team members feel safe voicing concerns, sharing ideas, and addressing challenges together. The *Frontiers in Psychology* study highlighted how these small, consistent actions with integrity build trust, creating a powerful platform for collaboration and innovation.

Unethical compromises breed distrust, skepticism, and uncertainty. Elizabeth Holmes and Theranos illustrate how a lack of transparency and accountability from leadership destroys trust among employees, investors, and customers. The broken trust fostered a toxic workplace, silencing dissent and innovation, leading to the company's failure.

Positive examples of building and maintaining integrity, even during crises, provide a sharp contrast. Johnson & Johnson's handling of the 1982 Tylenol poisoning incident remains a hallmark of ethical leadership. The company prioritized public safety over short-term financial considerations, recalling over 31 million bottles of Tylenol and communicating with stakeholders (NewsHour et al., 2014). By acting with integrity and accountability, Johnson & Johnson not only restored public trust but also strengthened its brand's reputation in the long term.

A 2012 article in the *Journal of Business Ethics* called "*Authentic leadership and behavioral integrity as drivers of follower commitment and performance* reinforces the importance of trust in leadership" (Leroy et al., 2012). Ethical leaders who prioritize integrity foster environments where employees feel empowered to take risks, suggest ideas, and face challenges head-on. This culture of trust encourages resilience and innovation, enabling organizations to adapt to change and thrive in competitive markets. Knowing that their leaders act with their best interests in mind, employees in these environments are more likely to stay loyal and committed.

To build trust through integrity, leaders must:

Be transparent: Share the truth, even when it's uncomfortable. This openness creates a safe space for employees to communicate their concerns, suggestions, and feedback.

Follow through on promises: A leader's word must mean something. If circumstances change, communicate why and how you plan to adjust. Delivering on commitments is crucial to building long-term trust.

Lead by example: A leader's actions set the tone for the rest of the team. Demonstrating integrity in your decisions and behaviors encourages others to do the same.

Trust is as much of an ideal as a strategic advantage. Leaders who act with integrity foster environments where individuals and teams thrive, driving innovation and long-term organizational success. By embracing transparency, modeling accountability, and prioritizing trust, leaders create a legacy of resilience and collaboration that benefits employees, customers, and stakeholders alike.

The Importance of Transparency in Leadership

A key lesson from the Theranos scandal is the critical role transparency plays in leadership. For years, Elizabeth Holmes maintained a veil of secrecy around the true state of her company's technology. She presented a false image of success to investors, employees, and the public. This lack of transparency, among other things, led to the company's downfall. Without a clear and honest exchange of information, trust eroded, and the organization became vulnerable to collapse.

Transparency requires leaders to be open about their decision-making processes and share both successes and failures. Leaders being upfront about challenges not only fosters trust but also engages the team in problem-solving. Employees who understand the bigger picture are more invested in the organization's goals and more motivated to contribute to overcoming obstacles. Transparency makes people feel included and valued, while secrecy leaves them uncertain and disconnected.

Leaders choose secrecy breed an environment of doubt and fear. Employees left in the dark question their role and the organization's direction. This uncertainty leads to disengagement and low morale, which can affect the organization's overall performance.

Ethical leaders prioritize transparency. They admit when things aren't going according to plan and involve their teams in crafting solutions. This type of open leadership builds resilience and empowers team members to take initiative. Transparency as a core part of leadership encourages a culture of accountability, where individuals take ownership of their actions because they trust their leader to do the same.

Integrity and transparency are fundamentally connected. While integrity ensures that leaders remain true to their values, transparency ensures their teams remain informed and engaged. Together, these traits form the bedrock of trust within an organization. Leaders who uphold these principles create an environment where people can perform at their best, unencumbered by doubt, fear, or mistrust.

Building trust through integrity requires consistent ethical behavior and a commitment to an atmosphere of trust that allows their teams and organizations to thrive in the long term.

Navigating Ethical Dilemmas: Maintaining Authenticity in Challenging Situations

Every leader will face ethical dilemmas in his or her career. These situations often involve conflicting values, competing interests, or significant external pressures. Ethical dilemmas test a leader's commitment to maintaining integrity, especially when the stakes are high and the pressure to act intensifies. Navigating these dilemmas is a crucial part of maintaining authenticity and building long-term credibility as a leader.

Ethical dilemmas can take many forms, from addressing unfair treatment within a team to deciding whether to report an internal mistake that could harm the company's reputation. These situations often present no easy solutions, which is why they serve as genuine tests of leadership. How a leader responds in these moments not only reflects their personal values but also sets a powerful example for their team. Leaders prove their integrity and authenticity not in the simple times, but in the difficult times when they must make hard decisions under pressure.

To navigate these dilemmas with authenticity and integrity, leaders need to adopt a reflective approach. Here are a few essential steps to help you:

Pause and reflect: When faced with an ethical dilemma, taking a moment to pause and assess the situation is crucial. Rushing to a decision without considering the full context leads to compromised values or short-sighted solutions. Reflection allows you to identify what's at stake and how your actions will align with your core values. Ask yourself, "What is the ethical choice here, and does it reflect my principles?"

Consider all stakeholders: Ethical decisions don't just impact you as the leader—they affect employees, customers, shareholders, and the broader community. A leader must weigh the needs of all these groups and make decisions that respect the diverse perspectives involved. While pleasing everyone is not always possible, ethical leadership requires considering how decisions will affect various stakeholders and finding a solution that is fair and just.

Seek counsel: No one expects leaders to have all the answers, especially in complex situations. Consulting with trusted advisors or mentors provides valuable insights and fresh perspectives. Ethical dilemmas often come with blind spots and reaching out to others helps you gain a more comprehensive understanding of the issue. Getting input from people who may have faced similar challenges can help you navigate the situation more effectively.

Be transparent: Authentic leadership requires honesty and openness, especially when dealing with ethical dilemmas. Explaining the rationale behind the decision to the team is important. Sharing the process fosters trust and shows that the leader values transparency even when the decisions are difficult. This approach prioritizes and encourages ethical decision-making.

Let's consider an example: A leader faces the choice of short-cuts on a project to save time and money. The pressure to meet deadlines and deliver results intensifies, but an ethical leader, guided by their core value of integrity, refuses to compromise on quality. This leader understands that maintaining standards is essential to building long-term trust with stakeholders even if it means delaying the project or incurring higher costs. This decision to prioritize quality over expedience communicates the organization's commitment to excellence and its refusal to compromise integrity for short-term gains.

In this scenario, the leader's authenticity shines through. By staying true to their values and refusing to take short-cuts, they reinforce the organization's ethical standards and earn the respect of their team and clients. While the short-term consequences might be challenging, the long-term benefits—of credibility, and a reputation for integrity are invaluable.

Navigating ethical dilemmas with integrity is never easy, but it's where authentic leadership is most clearly defined. Leaders who remain steadfast in their values, even in difficult situations, set themselves apart and create environments where integrity is not just a principle, but a practice. In the end, these are the decisions that build lasting success.

The Ripple Effect of Ethical Leadership

Leading with integrity has a profound impact that goes far beyond the immediate situation or decision. When a leader models ethical behavior, they create a standard of conduct that permeates the entire organization. Ethical leadership sets the tone for how employees interact with one another, approach challenges, and engage with clients, stakeholders, and the community. This ripple effect strengthens organizational culture and drives long-term success.

Not only did a 2012 article in the *Journal of Business Ethics* find that leaders who prioritize integrity and transparency build a thriving environment that encourages innovation, but it also found that when employees perceive their leaders as ethical, they are more motivated to contribute, take calculated risks, and collaborate more effectively, thus strengthening the overall cohesion of the organization and empowering teams to excel (Leroy et al., 2012).

Ethical leadership affects all levels of the organization. When leaders show ethical decision-making, they show employees that integrity matters more than short-term gains. This inspires employees to emulate those values, creating a culture of honesty, transparency, and accountability. As the *Journal of Business Ethics* emphasizes, the result is a workplace environment where individuals feel safe to innovate and share ideas because they know they are valuable contributors who are supported by their leadership. They trust their leaders will listen to their concerns and reward ethical behavior. This creates a culture of trust, where collaboration, innovation, and resilience thrive. Trust in leadership also fosters long-term loyalty, helping organizations navigate challenges and build sustainable success.

The opposite is also true. Leaders who compromise their integrity, even in small ways, create a dangerous precedent. A 2012 study in the *Journal of Business Ethics* found that ethical leadership affects employee behaviors, such as job performance and organizational citizenship.(Leroy et al., 2012) Leaders who fail to act with integrity weaken trust and foster environments where unethical behavior becomes normalized. This was clear with Theranos, where Elizabeth Holmes' deceptive practices led to a toxic culture of fear and secrecy. Employees, discouraged from raising concerns, watched as the lack of transparency and accountability allowed systemic issues to go unchecked, leading to the company's collapse.

Ethical leadership also enhances the organization's reputation with external stakeholders. Trustworthy partnerships result from companies prioritizing integrity and accountability, which strengthens customer relationships and provides a competitive edge. Ethical leadership resonates with employees and clients and provides a significant advantage in today's era of increasing corporate responsibility.

By modeling integrity, leaders create an environment where teams thrive, innovation flourishes, and trust drives success. In doing so, they not only strengthen their organization from within but also position it for enduring success in a competitive, ever-changing business landscape.

Accountability and Trust

Integrity and accountability go hand in hand. A leader's effectiveness relies on their readiness to take responsibility for their actions, decisions, and outcomes. This includes both successes and mistakes. True accountability means owning your choices, standing by them, and learning from them, regardless of the outcome.

Accountability is about personal ownership, where leaders not only ensure their team's work is on track, on task, and meeting goals, but they also take responsibility for the outcomes, regardless of whether they hit the mark or not. This kind of accountability creates an atmosphere of trust and transparency within an organization. When a leader models accountability, they set a powerful example for everyone, inspiring team members to adopt the same level of responsibility in their roles.

Having no accountability can have disastrous consequences, as seen with Theranos. Elizabeth Holmes, the once-revered CEO, failed to acknowledge critical errors in the company's technology and decision-making. Instead of being upfront about the issues, she suppressed dissent and pushed forward with deceptive tactics. This lack of accountability created a toxic environment where employees felt silenced and demoralized, and the lack of transparency allowed problems to compound. The ripple effect of Holmes' actions devastated not just her company, but also the trust of her investors, employees, and the public.

Companies lacking accountability often create a culture where disengagement, fear, and failure flourish. When leaders don't admit mistakes or take responsibility, they show their team that honesty and transparency aren't important. This discourages employees from raising concerns, speaking transparently, or pushing for change. The lack of accountability harms the entire organization, not just the leader.

On the flip side, when leaders show integrity by embracing accountability, they send a coherent message that ownership matters. Leaders who step up to admit that they are wrong or that something needs to be thought about differently show that they are driven by a commitment to doing what's best for the team and the organization, not by their egos. This honesty strengthens trust between leaders and their teams and fosters an environment where mistakes are learning opportunities, not failures.

When employees see their leaders holding themselves accountable, they feel empowered to do the same. This ownership spreads, fostering a culture of individual responsibility and motivating everyone to contribute to organizational success. Accountability motivates people by showing that leadership values and supports their efforts and encourages innovation and risk-taking while solidifying commitment to the project and organization

Accountability also helps teams build resilience. When leaders acknowledge challenges and mistakes, the team can address issues head-on and course-correct quickly. Leaders who avoid accountability may attempt to cover up problems or delay addressing them, which can lead to bigger consequences down the line. In contrast, leaders who take ownership of missteps enable the team to bounce back stronger and more effectively. This resilience, built on accountability, is key to thriving in fast-paced, ever-evolving business environments.

Accountability also means delivering on promises, and not just about owning up to what went wrong. Following through on commitments is a critical part of leadership credibility. When a leader says they'll do something, and they do it, they build trust. The lack of commitment shown when a leader doesn't follow through on a promise causes team members to question their integrity, which leads to distrust. Accountable leaders remain grounded and reliable, thus showing the team the trustworthiness of their word.

In organizations where accountability thrives, employees are more likely to take initiative, contribute creative solutions, and push the boundaries of what's possible. They aren't afraid to speak up or admit mistakes because they know their leaders have their backs and will work with them, and not around them, to find solutions.

Accountability forms the backbone of trust. Without it, even the best-intentioned leaders cannot earn their team's confidence. With it, leaders not only build credibility but also create a workplace culture where integrity, collaboration, and trust are the norms. Leaders who take ownership of their actions create an environment where everyone feels responsible for the collective success of the organization.

Leading with integrity may not always provide immediate rewards, but doing so builds long-term success. When leaders prioritize honesty, transparency, and accountability, they foster trust and loyalty among their teams, customers, and stakeholders.

Authentic leadership requires the courage to make tough decisions, admit mistakes, and prioritize ethics over convenience. In doing so, leaders not only ensure their own success but also create resilient organizations that are innovative and built on trust.

Creating an Ethical Organizational Culture

At Theranos, Elizabeth Holmes fostered a culture of fear and secrecy, discouraging employees to speak up. This toxic environment prevented critical issues from being addressed, ultimately leading to the company's collapse. In contrast,

Leadership sets the tone for the culture of any organization. A leader's values, actions, and decision-making processes influence the behavior of employees at every level. Whereas Elizabeth Holmes created a culture of fear and secrecy by silencing those who spoke up, which prevented critical issues from being addressed, and ultimately the downfall of Theranos, leaders who promote an ethical organizational culture create an environment where employees feel empowered to share their ideas, raise concerns, and contribute meaningfully. Consider a company that recognizes employees who show ethical behavior as part of its employee recognition program. By highlighting these actions, the company reinforces integrity and encourages others to follow suit. This approach not only motivates individuals but also builds a cohesive, value-driven culture based on strong ethics.

Several foundational elements build an ethical organizational culture:

Clear communication of values: Leaders must consistently articulate the organization's values and integrate them into every aspect of its operations. This clarity helps employees understand the ethical standards expected of them.

Recruitment and training: Hiring individuals who align with the organization's values is key. Training programs focused on ethics and decision-making reinforce these values and ensure that employees know how to apply them in their daily work.

Recognition and reward systems: Recognizing and rewarding ethical behavior signals its importance within the organization.

Employees who see ethical actions being rewarded are more likely to act with integrity themselves.

Safe channels for reporting unethical conduct: Providing employees with safe, confidential channels for reporting unethical behavior without fear of retaliation is essential. This transparency fosters accountability and helps maintain an ethical organizational climate.

Ethical Leadership in Crisis Management

The genuine test of a leader's integrity often comes during times of crisis. Whether it's a financial downturn, a public relations issue, or an internal conflict, how leaders respond in these moments defines their organization's future. During a crisis, ethical leadership becomes not just important, but essential.

We saw this during the COVID pandemic. Leaders at every level were tested. Faced with unprecedented uncertainty, many leaders had to make swift decisions that would affect the lives of their employees, customers, and communities. Ethical leaders navigated the crisis by prioritizing transparency, accountability, and empathy, setting themselves apart and earning trust in a time of widespread fear and confusion.

Transparency became an important tenant of trust during the pandemic. Ethical leaders communicated openly with their stakeholders, providing clear, accurate, and timely information about how the crisis was affecting their business and the steps they were taking to address everything. This openness not only mitigated the negative effects of the crisis but also fostered a sense of calm and direction. Leaders who were honest about their challenges, whether it was financial strain or supply chain disruptions, were better able to maintain trust with their teams and customers.

Accountability also came to the forefront. Ethical leaders don't shy away from tough decisions or conversations. They take responsibility for their actions and sacrifice to uphold their values and protect their people. Leaders who were accountable for their pandemic response and acknowledged mistakes or missteps along the way were more likely to sustain long-term loyalty from employees and customers alike. In contrast, those who avoided accountability or placed blame elsewhere saw their reputations suffer.

One prime example is how organizations navigated the shift to remote work during COVID. At the time, many companies didn't even have a work-from-home policy. Ethical leaders who were honest about the challenges, stayed connected to what employees needed, and stayed flexible as policies evolved built stronger trust and collaboration, even across fully remote teams.

Empathy was perhaps the most humanizing aspect of ethical leadership during the pandemic. Ethical leaders stayed connected to the real, personal impact the crisis was having on their employees, customers, and broader community. Decisions were about people, not just about numbers on a balance sheet. Authentic leaders showed empathy by offering flexibility, support, and understanding towards those affected by the crisis. This emphasized that ethical leadership involves more than just making business decisions; it also entails doing the right thing for people.

Crises don't just test a leader's tactical abilities—they test their moral compass. Consider the example of a company facing a significant product recall. An ethical leader addresses the issue head-on, communicates openly with customers and stakeholders, and takes full responsibility for the problem. By prioritizing transparency and accountability, even amid a crisis, that leader strengthens their organization's reputation and trustworthiness.

The COVID pandemic taught us that crisis situations create opportunities for leaders to reinforce their commitment to integrity. When leaders handle crises with honesty, responsibility, and empathy, they not only navigate the immediate challenges but also foster resilience and loyalty that will endure long after the crisis has passed.

Practical Steps for Enhancing Ethical Leadership

To further solidify the concepts discussed, here are practical steps that leaders can take to enhance their ethical leadership:

1. **Develop a Personal Code of Ethics:** Leaders should take the time to clearly define their own ethical principles. This personal code of ethics acts as a guide in difficult situations and helps ensure consistency in decision-making.

2. **Promote Open Dialogue:** Encourage an environment where team members feel comfortable discussing ethical concerns without fear of retribution. Open dialogue promotes transparency and can uncover potential issues before they become significant problems.

3. **Lead by example:** Actions speak louder than words. Leaders must consistently show ethical behavior in their actions and decisions. This sets a powerful example for others to follow.

4. **Invest in Ethics Training:** Regular training on ethical decision-making helps employees at all levels understand integrity and how to apply ethical principles in their daily work.

5. **Establish Clear Policies:** Organizations should have clear policies and procedures that outline expected ethical behaviors and the consequences of unethical actions. These policies provide a framework for maintaining high ethical standards.

6. **Foster a Supportive Culture:** Building a culture that supports ethical behavior requires ongoing effort. Recognize and reward ethical behavior and ensure safe channels for reporting unethical conduct.

7. **Evaluate and Reflect:** Regularly evaluate the ethical climate of the organization and reflect on areas for improvement. This

continuous process helps to keep ethical considerations at the forefront of organizational priorities.

By implementing these steps, leaders can reinforce their commitment to integrity and create an organizational environment where ethical behavior is the norm.

Final Thoughts: Ethical Leadership, Trust, and Accountability

Navigating ethical dilemmas and leading with accountability are two sides of the same coin in leadership. Both test a leader's commitment to integrity, especially when the stakes are high. Whether faced with a tough decision that challenges personal values or taking ownership of a mistake, ethical leaders understand that their influence shapes not only their team but also the culture of the entire organization.

Ethical leadership demands that leaders be both transparent and accountable, even when it's uncomfortable. This transparency builds trust, while accountability fosters a culture where everyone feels responsible for their work and the overall success of the organization. Leaders who embrace these principles inspire their teams to do the same, creating a ripple effect where integrity, trust, and collaboration become the norm.

Crises, like the COVID pandemic, reveal the measure of a leader's true integrity. Ethical leaders who respond to crisis with empathy, honesty, and responsibility are better positioned to guide their organizations through uncertainty and emerge stronger on the other side. These leaders don't shy away from tough conversations, and they don't compromise their values for short-term gains. Instead, they embrace the challenge, knowing that integrity will lead them to long-term success.

Leading with integrity and accountability is about making the right choices and setting an example that inspires others to do the same. Leaders who commit to these principles cultivate a resilient, innovative, and ethical culture that drives sustainable success.

5

Authentic Communication

Authentic communication is the ability to convey messages which gives effective leadership its strength with intention and what gives effective leadership its strength while creating an atmosphere of trust and collaboration. When leaders communicate authentically, they set the stage for meaningful relationships, foster transparency, and cultivate an environment where team members feel heard and valued. Authentic communication goes beyond conveying information and allows connection on a deeper level, ensuring that the message resonates and motivates those involved.

In today's fast-paced world, leaders face the constant challenge of balancing directness with empathy. Authentic communication is honest and direct and is also considerate of the emotions and perspectives of others. This chapter underscores the need for authentic communication in establishing trust, and psychological safety. When leaders master this balance, they can create an environment where individuals are not afraid to speak up, share their ideas, or voice their concerns.

Authentic communication includes more than just spoken words; it also involves listening and providing meaningful feedback. Listening holds immense power. It transforms communication into a two-way street. True listening requires setting aside preconceived notions, being present in the moment, and striving to understand the other person. Through active listening, leaders gain insights into their team's needs, aspirations, and potential roadblocks, enabling them to make better decisions and build stronger relationships.

This chapter will also explore practical ways to cultivate an authentic communication style and highlight self-awareness, adaptability, and empathy. We will explore strategies to improve listening skills and create a feedback culture that encourages open dialogue and empowers everyone to contribute. By embracing these elements of authentic communication, leaders can not only enhance their effectiveness but also inspire their teams to achieve collective goals.

Authentic communication is about building bridges that connect people, ideas, and goals. It is about creating a leadership approach that is not only effective but also deeply empathetic, and that transforms a group of individuals into a cohesive, motivated team. Let's dive into the art of communicating with authenticity and explore how doing so can transform your leadership journey.

The Harmony of Directness and Empathy

Balancing directness and empathy is essential for creating psychological safety. Research by Amy Edmondson, a Harvard professor and pioneer in psychological safety, highlights that teams perform best when individuals feel safe to express themselves without fear of criticism or judgment (A. Edmondson, 1999). Edmondson defined psychological safety as "a shared belief that the team is safe for interpersonal risk-taking." This concept resonates deeply with the idea of authentic communication.

When leaders foster psychological safety, they create an environment where team members feel empowered to voice their concerns, offer feedback, and contribute new ideas. Edmondson's research reveals that teams with high psychological safety experience greater collaboration and creativity. (A. Edmondson & Lei, 2014) Conversely, teams that lack this safety often struggle with suppressed ideas, reduced engagement, and an atmosphere of fear that stifles innovation.

Consider a situation where a team member makes a mistake that affects a project deadline. In an environment without psychological safety, that individual might try to cover up the error out of fear of being reprimanded, which could exacerbate the problem. However, in a team that prioritizes psychological safety, the individual feels comfortable admitting the mistake early, allowing the team to address it quickly and collaboratively. This openness minimizes risks and strengthens trust within the team.

For leaders, creating psychological safety requires a deliberate effort to balance clarity and empathy in communication. Edmondson's findings highlight how delivery of feedback directly affects a team member's willingness to engage and take ownership of their work. Delivering constructive feedback, for example, should not only focus on the areas for improvement but should also acknowledge the individual's efforts and contributions. Instead of feeling like a personal critique, this approach positions feedback as a chance for improvement.

Psychological safety pertains to how leaders communicate and how they listen. By actively listening and responding empathetically, leaders signal to team members that their thoughts and feelings are valuable. Leaders who cultivate this culture build stronger relationships, reduce defensiveness, and encourage open dialogue, even in challenging situations. Not only did Edmondson's research focus on how feedback is delivered, but she also underscored that leaders must actively maintain psychological safety through consistent actions that reinforce trust.

By integrating empathy into direct communication, leaders create an environment where individuals feel respected and valued, even in tough conversations. This fosters a culture of psychological safety, enabling teams to thrive and innovate without fear of failure. The harmony of directness and empathy are leadership philosophies that build resilience and drives success across teams and organizations.

Balancing Directness with Autonomy: A Leadership Challenge

Leadership requires navigating the tricky balance inherent in direct communication, which can sometimes feel like giving orders, and providing full autonomy to a team to work through a challenge on their own. It's easy to subscribe to the notion that being clear in your messaging is the best way to provide directions to a team, but the more experience I have gained the more I have realized that giving direction isn't always the best way. In fact, it can sometimes impede the team's creativity and growth.

In my experience, allowing the team to generate their own solutions is sometimes more beneficial than providing one. Of course, there are times you need to be decisive and give clear direction, especially when deadlines are looming or the stakes are high. But I've also seen firsthand how people grow when they have the space to figure things out for themselves. Empowering the team to solve problems builds their confidence, encourages more creative thinking, and strengthens their sense of ownership over the results.

This balance can be the ultimate struggle. The urge exists to provide the solution because it often feels quicker. Knowing when to be direct versus when to step back is key to authentic leadership. Mastering this takes time. The more I've practiced stepping back, the more I've seen the benefits of letting the team navigate their own way. Not only does this boost their morale but also leads to better, more innovative results in the long run. I've learned, that being a good leader means understanding when your team needs direction and when they just need your trust. Finding that balance creates a space where people can thrive, knowing they're supported but also trusted to deliver on their own.

Cultivating an Authentic Communication Style

Find your authentic communication style by figuring out what feels right for you—not by mimicking someone else. Your authentic voice should reflect your values, strengths, and beliefs. This idea aligns with the foundation of authentic leadership theory, which emphasizes self-awareness, an internalized moral perspective, and relational transparency as key traits (Avolio & Gardner, 2005). So, how do you do that? Let's walk through some simple steps to help you develop a style that's both effective and true to who you are, with your moral compass as your guide.

Get Clear About What You Believe In: Before anything else, you need to know your core values. These are the principles that steer your actions and decisions. Consider things like honesty, transparency, and empathy. Once you're clear on those, your communication style will naturally align with them. When challenges pop up, your moral compass will help keep you grounded, ensuring your words match your beliefs. Ask yourself:

1. What values do I want my communication to reflect?
2. How do I stay true to those values, even under pressure?

Check Your Surroundings—Culture and Industry Matter: While staying true to your values is key, you also need to consider the environment you're working in. Company culture, industry norms, and expectations affect how people receive messages. For example, a corporate setting may call for more formal and direct communication, whereas creative industries might appreciate a more flexible and casual approach. Understanding these nuances helps you adapt without losing your authenticity. Think about:

1. What's the communication culture like in my company or in my industry?
2. How can I adjust my style to fit in without losing what makes me unique?

Know Your Strengths (and Your Blind Spots): Everyone has strengths in communication—whether it's being empathetic, direct, or somewhere in between. Embrace what feels natural to you. And be honest enough to acknowledge where you might struggle. Maybe you shy away from confrontation or find delivering tough feedback difficult to do. Develop your strengths while also focusing on your weaknesses.

1. Recall effective communication instances; what ensured success?
2. Be honest: Where could you improve? More directness? A little extra empathy?

Adapt to Your Audience Without Losing Yourself: Tailoring your style to different situations—whether it's a one-on-one chat, a big team meeting, or a high-stakes presentation is important. Nevertheless, preserve your distinctive voice and style. Your moral compass will keep you grounded, which helps you adapt your tone and delivery while staying true to your values.

1. Consider your audience: What do they need—reassurance, motivation, or clarity?
2. Adjust your approach, but make sure your core beliefs still shine through.

Balance Directness with Empathy: There's a fine line between being direct and being empathetic. Both are important. Directness provides clarity and efficiency, while empathy builds trust and connection. The real magic happens when you can strike that balance, especially during tough conversations. Let your moral compass guide you in figuring out how much directness or empathy the moment calls for.

1. Before giving feedback, ask yourself: How can I be both clear and compassionate?
2. Your values should direct your choices: directness versus empathy.

Really Listen: Remember, authentic communication is about talking *and* listening. Active listening shows people you value what they have to say, which builds trust and connection. Plus, when you listen carefully, your responses will be more thoughtful and aligned with your values.

1. Focus on understanding the other person's point of view before responding.
2. Reflect on what you've heard to ensure clarity, then respond authentically.

Let Your Moral Compass Guide You: The moral compass is your North Star. Whether you're delivering feedback, leading a team, or handling a tough conversation, your communication should reflect who you are at your core. Use your compass to stay aligned with your beliefs, even when the pressure is on.

1. Before important conversations, ask: Is what I'm about to say in line with my values?
2. Afterward, reflect by asking yourself: Did I stay true to who I am?

The Art of Listening: Creating a Culture of Open Dialogue

Strong leadership relies on the crucial skill of effective listening. Effective communication involves more than passive listening; it requires grasping the underlying meaning, emotion, and expectations of what is being said. Effective listening involves full engagement, thoughtful responses, and openness to learning.

In authentic communication, listening is key to helping you connect with your team on a deeper level. By listening, you get a better sense of what's driving your people, their concerns, their hopes, and their ideas. That kind of understanding builds trust, which leads to better decision-making and, ultimately, a stronger, more engaged team.

The key is that listening involves a mindset of humility and receptiveness to others' views. Listening is an active process. You're not just sitting passively letting things go in one ear and out the other. You're absorbing, processing, and opening up to perspectives that might challenge your own. Active listening makes people feel valued. That's what builds trust and creates a space where open, honest conversations can happen.

One of the biggest benefits of listening is that it helps you catch things that might not be obvious. Maybe someone hesitates before responding to a deadline in a meeting. That hesitation could be a sign of deeper concerns about the timeline. If you're tuned in and pick up on it, you can address the hesitation right away instead of letting it fester and create bigger problems down the line.

Listening also empowers your team. When you take the time to hear someone out without jumping in or trying to solve their problem for them, you're giving them ownership of their ideas. That's huge for morale because you're showing that their input matters and that they have a real stake in the outcome.

In times of conflict, listening can be your best tool. Misunderstandings fuel conflicts. The willingness to listen without judgment goes a long way in resolving or avoiding conflicts all together. When people feel heard, they more easily find solutions that respect everyone's needs and feelings. This builds stronger relationships in the long run.

Non-verbal cues also play a big role in listening. Sometimes it's what's *not* being said that gives you the most insight. A team member might say they're fine with a decision, but their body language—maybe crossed arms or avoiding eye contact—tells a different story. As a leader, your job is to notice those signals and dig a little deeper to make sure everyone is on board.

Listening helps you grow as a leader. It offers an unconsidered new perspective. This openness sparks innovation and encourages people to share their ideas. And that's where the best, most creative solutions come from.

Types of Listening

Being a good listener is one of the hardest skills to master, especially in leadership, when juggling so many responsibilities can be tasking.

There are three main types of listening:
Active, Reflective, and Empathetic.

Active Listening: This involves giving full attention to the speaker, acknowledging their message, and responding thoughtfully. Active listening shows you value the speaker's input and are interested in what they have to say.

Reflective Listening: Reflective listening goes a step further by summarizing or paraphrasing what the speaker has said to confirm understanding. This not only ensures clarity but also makes the speaker feel heard and validated.

Empathetic Listening: Empathetic listening focuses on understanding the speaker's emotions and perspective. It is important when dealing with sensitive issues or providing support during challenging times.

We can all use a little work on at least one of them. Which one requires your greatest attention?

Unlocking "Listening Expert Mode"

Mastering these three types of listening isn't about moving from one stage to the next but about layering them together to become more skilled and versatile in communication.

Think of it like leveling up in listening:

Beginner Mode: In the beginning, a leader may focus on just one type of listening—active listening. At this stage, the goal is to be present, attentive, and responsive. This foundational skill ensures the speaker feels acknowledged and establishes basic understanding.

Intermediate Mode: As listening skills develop, a leader might use two types of listening together, often combining active and reflective listening. They prioritize clear communication, focusing on both understanding and summarizing spoken content. This deepens engagement and helps avoid misunderstandings.

Expert Mode: At the most advanced level, leaders engage with all three types of listening—active, reflective, and empathetic—simultaneously. This means they are present, ensuring clarity by reflecting on what they've heard, while also tuning into the emotional undertones of the conversation. This level of listening creates the deepest connections, builds trust, and leads to the most meaningful outcomes.

Why We Stink at Listening

Let's face it—most of us aren't superb listeners. Leaders, in particular, face a lot of barriers that impede effective listening like distractions, preconceived notions, and time constraints. These obstacles prevent us from engaging with others, leaving conversations incomplete or misunderstood. So, what can we do about it?

To overcome these barriers, it's essential to:

Minimize Distractions: We live in a world full of distractions, whether it's the constant ping of devices or a never-ending to-do list. Effective listening requires being present. Put the phone down, close the laptop, and focus on the person in front of you.

Challenge Assumptions: We all carry preconceived notions that influence how we listen. It's easy to think we already know what someone is going to say. However, when we approach conversations with an open mind and set aside judgments, we open ourselves to new insights and better connections.

Direct Communication: While direct communication is valuable for clarity and setting expectations, it can sometimes limit the depth of conversation, especially if it's too blunt or rushed. Being direct has its place, but leaders need to balance directness with empathy and open dialogue to avoid shutting down the conversation or missing important nuances.

Allocate Time for Listening: One of the biggest challenges leaders face is time. There's always something pulling your attention in another direction. Sometimes being limited on time causes brevity. That's why setting aside dedicated time for meaningful conversations is important.

Communicating When Time Is Limited

In the fast-paced world of leadership, time is often the one resource we can't stretch. Juggling meetings, deadlines, and unexpected crises pull leaders in different directions. When time is short, we're forced to make quick decisions and communicate even quicker. In these moments, the balance between being efficient and remaining authentic becomes crucial.

There's no denying that in the rush of a busy day, conversations often become shortened. You might deliver a message in 30 seconds that deserves five minutes or wrap-up a discussion before it feels complete. Instead of condensing what you say, adapt the delivery to fit in a tighter window of time without losing the core of what matters.

Sometimes, brevity is a necessary skill. Knowing when to give just enough information to move things forward while holding off on the deeper dive for later is an art in itself. As a leader, there's a constant tug-of-war: do you lean into the directness of getting things done, or pause to show empathy and engage at a deeper level? In these moments, clarity can be your ally, but so can a well-placed word of acknowledgment.

The trick with communication in these short, intense moments is knowing that not everything needs to be unpacked right away. Sometimes, the best leadership move is to provide a general direction and let the team figure out the finer details. You're not shirking responsibility or withholding information. Instead, you're trusting your team's ability to fill in the blanks. As a leader, you can offer guidance without the need to spell everything out. Giving others space to draw their own conclusions is empowering.

That said, not all leaders find striking this balance to be easy. I remember my time as an intern in the customer service department for a major elevator and escalator company in Toledo, Ohio. The interns worked under the Executive Vice President of Customer Service, who we'll call Rod. As interns, our work involved data entry, analysis, and call center support — typical entry-level tasks. Whenever I had a question, needed guidance, or just wanted to spend more time learning from Rod, I would approach him at his office to ask if he had a few minutes to talk. Rod invariably answered, "I have more than just a few minutes. I have all the time you need!"

This had a major impact on me and my leadership style today. It's clear to me now that even though Rod didn't actually have the time in his schedule that he gave to me, he made time to talk with me. Taking time for people, even in a fast-paced environment, is what separates the prominent leaders from the mediocre. I can still see his office today, how he would close his laptop, point for me to pull up a chair, and dedicate his full attention to my question. Rod's approach was rare, but it shouldn't be. Rod exemplifies the ideal leader who values potential above temporal constraints.

I will admit that pausing the workday like Rod did is not always possible. There will be times when brevity leads to confusion or misinterpretation, and that's okay. What matters is that you create a space for follow-up when needed. Set the stage for ongoing dialogue, even if today's conversation has to be cut short. I like to acknowledge the time constraint, offer to schedule more time to continue the conversation, and follow up with the person in these situations. Being short on time is a temporary obstacle. We can always find time for important conversations.

Accepting that conversation can't always finish in the first attempt, or that there isn't always enough time to say everything might be the hardest part. By following up and completing those conversations, you elevate your leadership abilities. Many leaders neglect completing conversations. Committing to returning and finishing what you started will elevate your communication skills and leadership.

Fostering a Feedback-Rich Environment

Creating a culture where feedback flows is fundamental to the growth of both individuals and teams. Feedback, when shared and received with a genuine spirit of improvement and mutual respect, turns challenges into opportunities for growth. Building this type of environment requires intentionality.

Encourage Constructive Feedback: As leaders, modeling the behavior you want to see by giving and receiving feedback in a respectful, constructive way is important. Cultivate an environment that values and encourages feedback by having regular check-ins or feedback sessions create safe spaces for open dialogue. This openness encourages others to share their thoughts without fear.

Receiving Feedback with Openness: If you're like me, receiving feedback can be tough sometimes. Viewing it as a gift, rather than a critique, shifts your mindset. Active listening, reflecting on the feedback, and showing gratitude make the process more comfortable for everyone. Since nobody is perfect, feedback is one of the best tools we have to keep improving.

Building Feedback Mechanisms: Having structured feedback mechanisms, like regular feedback sessions, anonymous surveys, or 360-degree feedback processes, can help make feedback a part of the team's natural rhythm. When feedback becomes part of the routine, having meaningful exchanges that build trust and development within the team is easier.

Final Thoughts: The Impact of Authentic Communication

The ripple effects of authentic communication within an organization are profound. Here are four key effects I've experienced:

Building Trust: Integrity and reliability build authentic communication. When you communicate honestly, you enhance trust and security in your team. People know where they stand with you, and that consistency creates a firm foundation for relationships.

Enhance Collaboration: Clear and open communication helps ensure everyone is on the same page. This prevents misunderstandings, aligns goals, and makes working together feel seamless. When we're clear with each other, collaboration becomes second nature.

Foster a Sense of Belonging: Empathy and openness in communication create a sense of inclusion and support. People feel valued and understood, which increases their engagement and motivation. When team members feel like they belong, they bring their best selves to work.

Drive Innovation: Open and honest communication creates an environment that values diverse ideas and perspectives, encourages people to share ideas, challenge the status quo, and think creatively. This environment of psychological safety allows innovation to thrive. When everyone feels safe, they're more willing to take risks, experiment, and contribute to continuous improvement.

Authentic communication transcends skill and requires continual practice. It takes a commitment to express yourself with integrity, listen intending to understand, and foster an environment where feedback is not just given, but welcomed. As you continue your leadership journey, remember that at the heart of authentic leadership lies the power of authentic communication—it's the bridge that connects, understands, and transforms.

6

Leading by Example

Leading by example is the epitome of authentic leadership. By embodying the values and principles you advocate for, you become a living testament to the ideals you wish to instill within your organization. This approach to leadership transcends the mere act of dictating policies and procedures and involves a deep commitment to living out the very values that you expect from your team. This chapter delves into the essence of modeling authentic behavior and explores the effects that such leadership can have on organizational culture.

Authentic behavior in leadership is as much a way of being as it is a set of actions. When leaders' actions align with their core values and beliefs, not only do they fortify their credibility and engender trust among their team members, but they also reinforce those values and inspire their teams to emulate these behaviors. This alignment between words and actions is crucial for building a culture of integrity and trust within the organization.

One of the most powerful aspects of leading by example is the way it shows values in action. For instance, a leader who prioritizes transparency must communicate openly and honestly, even when the news is not positive. This consistency builds a culture where team members feel safe to express their thoughts and concerns without fear of retribution. A leader who values collaboration must seek input from their team and be willing to listen and incorporate diverse perspectives. This behavior sets a standard for teamwork and mutual respect.

The power of authentic actions leads to one's ability to inspire and motivate others. Team members seeing their leaders living out the values they espouse creates a sense of purpose and direction. Employees readily embrace organizational vision and mission when witnessing their leader's commitment. This inspiration offers more than positive feelings and translates into higher levels of engagement and productivity. Individuals fully commit to the strategy and culture when they share a common goal and see their leaders behavior as genuine.

Bring Your Values to Life

Leading by example is about having the right intentions and showing up in your actions every single day. This gives you credibility and inspires others to follow. Let's dive into some practical strategies to help leaders live their values and inspire their teams by being the embodiment of those ideals. Here's how to bring your values into action:

Consistency in behavior: Consistency is paramount when leading by example. Make sure your actions always line up with your words. When you're consistent, people know what to expect from you. They know that what you say holds weight because your actions reflect those words.

Think of consistency like building a muscle. It requires a consistent, steadfast commitment to uphold the organization's values in everything you do, from making strategic decisions to interacting with your team daily. Let's say, for example, that you value ethical behavior. This means sticking to those ethical principles even when it's tough or when there's an easier, tempting shortcut available. Imagine facing a situation where taking a shortcut might yield short-term gains. Choosing the ethical path—even if it's slower or harder—sends a simple message to your team that integrity is non-negotiable.

Another example could be if you prioritize work-life balance for your team. Telling your employees to take time off but emailing them on weekends or working late hours yourself sends a mixed signal. Being consistent means respecting those boundaries and living out the values you advocate for. This alignment builds credibility and trust with your team.

Visibility and Accessibility: Visibility and accessibility are all about showing up and being approachable. Authentic leaders are the ones who leave the door to their office open 99% of the time. And when it's closed? It's for a confidential conversation, and that's okay. Outside of confidential moments, your office should be a place that invites everyone to feel welcome.

A big part of this is how you engage with your team. Limit the number of meetings you have in your office. Try holding them in more neutral spaces instead. Consider a conference room or flex space for the meeting. It's less intimidating, and puts everyone on a more equal footing, making people feel more comfortable to speak up.

Another example of being visible is being present around your workspace. Walk the floor, engage in casual conversations, ask about your team members' days. Visibility doesn't have to be a grand gesture. For instance, if there's a team meeting, don't just attend—take part. Be part of the conversation, not just the one running it. Let people see how you embody the values you're asking of them. Investing the time to build relationships will yield significant rewards.

Accountability and Ownership: Accountability is the epitome of authentic leadership. Leaders need to take responsibility for their actions, especially when things go sideways. Mistakes happen, but how we deal with them is what makes the difference. When leaders take ownership, it inspires similar behavior.

Imagine a scenario where a project falls short of its goals. As a leader, pointing fingers or making excuses is the easy path. Instead, an authentic example of accountability is stepping up, acknowledging what went wrong, and taking corrective steps. This not only builds trust within the team but also humanizes you as a leader. Show your team that you are someone who's willing to learn and improve, just like everyone else.

Sharing your learning moments is also part of taking ownership. If you've made a mistake, openly talking about the mistake and your own lessons learned will help your team feel more comfortable with their own setbacks. This encourages a culture where making mistakes is okay, provided there's a willingness to grow from them. By modeling accountability, you inspire your team members to own their work and create an environment that values and expects accountability.

Accountability also extends to giving credit where credit is due. Acknowledge the people who contributed to the success. This kind of ownership, where you share success and own failures is a powerful way to build trust and camaraderie within your team.

Make Leading by Example a Daily Practice

Leading by example is a daily practice that requires intentionality and effort. Consistency in behavior, visibility and accessibility, and accountability and ownership are the key strategies that help leaders put their values into action. What ties these strategies together is your own authenticity. Your team will detect insincerity. The power of leading by example comes from genuinely wanting to embody the values you preach.

These strategies emphasize genuine team interaction. When you're consistent, you show that your values aren't situational. Rather, they are principles you stand by. When you're visible and accessible, you break down barriers and make sure everyone knows they have a seat at the table. And when you're accountable, you show that even leaders are regular Joes, and making mistakes is okay as long as you own them and learn from them.

As you reflect on your leadership journey, ask yourself: Are you being consistent in living out your values, not just when it's easy, but also when it's tough? Are you visible and accessible in a way that makes your team feel they can reach you without hesitation? And are you owning your mistakes as well as celebrating the wins of others?

These are the everyday actions that define leadership by example. They might seem simple, but they require intentionality and practice. And remember, no one expects perfection. Be willing to grow, learn, and truly lead with authenticity. By keeping these strategies in mind and putting them into practice, you'll not only embody the values you care about, but also encourage your team to do the same.

Shape Norms and Expectations

Leading by example sets the template for what's acceptable and expected behavior within an organization. When leaders consistently act on values like respect, collaboration, and innovation, those values shape the culture. It doesn't take long for team members to pick up on these behaviors and start reflecting them in their own actions. This kind of alignment creates a positive, cohesive environment where everyone agrees and working towards the same goals.

Take, for instance, a leader who makes a commitment to diversity and inclusion by supporting diverse hiring practices and ensuring everyone has a voice. The team sees that these aren't just talking points or buzzwords; they're things that leadership truly values and practices. Over time, this commitment influences how teams decide, interact, and ultimately, how they succeed.

Reinforcement Through Recognition

Recognizing and rewarding value-driven behaviors is a powerful way to embed those values into the organization. Recognition can come in all shapes and sizes, from formal awards to a simple thank-you note.

Visualize a leader regularly acknowledging excellent teamwork and honesty, both in meetings and through personal messages. These actions motivate not just the individual being recognized but also set an example for others. Team members see what is important and everyone is encouraged to align their actions with those values.

One of the best examples I have seen comes from a friend and colleague. We can call him Fred. Fred has a quiet habit of sending handwritten thank-you notes to people across the organization. He writes to project managers, engineers, support staff, his boss, and even customers. He never announces the letters or checks in afterward to see if someone received one. He simply writes the note, drops it in the mail, and moves on.

The funny part is that his signature is almost unreadable. A looping scribble that could belong to anyone. For years, I have watched people receive these notes for the first time and have no idea who sent them. They usually ask around until someone says, "That is probably from Fred."

Most of us want to be sure the recipient knows we were the one who recognized them. Not Fred. For him, the value is in shining light on someone else, not in being seen as the one holding the flashlight. His anonymity does not dilute the impact. In many ways, it amplifies it. The message becomes less about the sender and more about the recipient's contribution.

I have seen those simple cards sit on desks and monitor stands for months. People keep them because they are reminders that someone noticed. Even without his name clearly attached, his care and the cultural signal behind it come through loud and clear.

This is the essence of reinforcement through recognition. When leaders acknowledge actions that reflect the organization's values, those actions spread. People understand what is celebrated, so they do more of it. Leaders who recognize others with authenticity help those values take deeper root in the culture.

The Broader Impact of Leading by Example

When leaders truly lead by example, the whole organization sees the ripple effects. The impact on immediate team dynamics also contributes to a wider culture of trust, integrity, and authenticity. This positive shift leads to higher employee engagement, better job satisfaction, and deeper loyalty. Ultimately, leading by example drives the organization's overall performance and success.

Enhance Employee Engagement and Job Satisfaction

Leading by example is one of the most powerful ways to boost employee engagement and job satisfaction. When team members see their leaders walking the talk by embodying the organization's values rather than just talking about them, they feel a stronger connection to the organization's mission and purpose. This connection has to be earned through genuine actions that show respect for your team and cannot be forced. Valued and proud employees are more engaged and satisfied with their jobs.

Authentic leaders create a work environment where employees feel satisfied. Successful leaders know that appreciated employees feel valued, heard, and seen. Even in situations where someone isn't satisfied, an authentic leader's duty involves promoting individual well-being, not solely company interests. A leader who cares for their people will help someone who feels out of place find a better fit, even if it's outside the company. This could mean tapping into your own network, providing referrals, or helping the employee transition into a new role that suits their skills and aspirations. Prioritize the person, not just the company's bottom line.

My Journey: Non-Competes

Be wary of companies that push non-competes. They often use them to protect an unhealthy work environment. Protecting a company's interests doesn't require restricting someone's livelihood. Instead, confidentiality agreements and non-solicitation clauses can protect company information while still respecting an employee's right to find a role where he or she feels fulfilled. If your organization uses non-competes to force people to stay instead of creating a culture that people want to be a part of, perhaps it's time to re-evaluate the culture itself.

Walking the Talk to Boost Engagement

When leaders lead by example, it sends a powerful message to the entire team. Go back to the example of a leader who emphasizes the importance of work-life balance. If that same leader practices what they preach by not sending late-night emails and encouraging people to disconnect during their time off, that consistency has a ripple effect. It shows that these aren't just words, but real values that shape how everyone works. Team members notice that kind of commitment, and it encourages them to prioritize their well-being as well, which contributes to greater job satisfaction.

Another way of leading by example is in the way you approach mistakes. When a leader owns their mistakes, they shows that failure isn't something to fear, but an opportunity to learn and grow. This kind of openness encourages employees to take initiative without the fear of being reprimanded for every little misstep and creates an environment where people feel safe to innovate, take risks, and grow—key ingredients for true engagement.

Creating a supportive work environment also means making sure people know their contributions matter. Recognition plays a huge role here. Simple acts like acknowledging someone's hard work during a meeting, writing a quick thank-you note, or celebrating team wins can do wonders for engagement. Noticing and appreciating employee efforts motivates people to excel.

Leaders should also be present and accessible. Whether it's having an open-door policy or taking the time to walk around and connect with team members, being visible matters because employees see that their leader is genuinely interested in them—not just as workers, but as individuals. And if an employee is struggling or needs support, accessibility means they feel comfortable approaching their leader for help.

Ultimately, enhancing employee engagement and satisfaction is about creating a place where people genuinely want to be. Lead with empathy, be consistent in your actions, and care enough to help each individual find the right fit whether that's in your team or somewhere else. When you create an environment that values authenticity and well-being, employees are more likely to feel proud, connected, and engaged in their work. And when that happens, everyone wins.

Leading by example allows you to create an environment where everyone feels committed to shared success. When leaders model the behaviors they expect from their team, they create a culture of excellence and accountability that drives performance at every level. This approach sets the stage for higher productivity, innovation, and a collective commitment to success that becomes embedded in the organization's DNA.

Organizations must ensure that all members share performance goals and metrics for success not only for individuals, but also for the team, including leadership. All goals should be interconnected and visible so everyone knows the organization's weekly wins and losses. This transparency creates a sense of unity and helps team members see how their efforts directly contribute to the larger objectives.

Imagine working in a company where every team meeting starts with a clear update on whether the organization is on track with its goals. There's no guessing, no surprises—just a clear understanding of where things stand. When leaders are transparent about both successes and setbacks, everyone is encouraged to rally together. Performance transforms into a team effort rather than an individual burden. Each employee should feel like they have a hand on the oar, rowing alongside their colleagues and their leader, knowing that everyone is pulling in the same direction.

Accountability becomes much more attainable when leadership is authentic and transparent. Authentic leaders make it clear what the goals are, why they matter, and what success looks like. They share their own progress, their own challenges, and their own wins. This openness removes ambiguity and ensures everyone works toward the same outcomes. Vague objectives and shifting targets disappear. The team defines everything, shares performance, and each member understands his or her role in achieving the team's goals.

Leading by example means being just as accountable as anyone else on the team. When leaders set high standards for themselves, they clarify that accountability starts at the top. For example, if the organization misses a target, an authentic leader doesn't shift the blame. They accept responsibility, discussing failures and outlining their path forward. This kind of leadership sets the standard for the rest of the team, demonstrating that accountability is a shared value rather than something to be feared.

Another aspect of driving organizational performance is the concept of shared success. Authentic leaders cultivate a culture where everyone celebrates success together. There are no lone wolves getting all the credit because everyone's contribution matters. When a team reaches a milestone, acknowledge the entire group that made things possible, not just the person who led the group. Authentic leaders recognize that success is a group effort, and they make sure that each team member feels valued for their part. This recognition not only boosts morale but also motivates everyone to keep striving towards shared goals.

When leaders commit to leading by example, they set a high standard for performance and create a culture of excellence and a commitment to continuous improvement. A leader who shows a relentless pursuit of quality and innovation sets a tone for the entire organization. They invest in their team's development, provide opportunities for learning, and clarity that growth is a priority.

This focus on continuous improvement becomes a driving force for organizational success. Team members, witnessing their leader's dedication to excellence, are similarly motivated. In this environment, everyone feels empowered to innovate, improve, and contribute to the organization's goals. Recognizing and valuing employee contributions makes them more likely to take ownership of their work, suggest new ideas, and improve processes.

In a high-performing culture, there are no surprises. Everyone knows the goals, everyone knows how they're doing, and everyone is accountable. Leaders who embody these principles create an environment where team members feel motivated to excel because they understand their role in the larger picture. Everyone feels a shared sense of ownership that surpasses individual tasks. They're invested in organizational success and understand that group wins translate to individual wins.

My Journey: Setting Personal Growth Goals

A shared vision and leading by example isn't only about hitting business goals. It's about unlocking the full potential of the people working toward them. When individuals see that their personal growth matters just as much as performance metrics, they begin to show up differently. They're more engaged, more curious, and more invested in the mission. That's why I make personal development a key part of everyone's goal-setting process. Doing this isn't just for show, either. Making personal development as important as professional development has a distinct purpose.They say lifelong learning keeps you young, and honestly, I believe it—because when people feel like they're growing, they show up with more energy, purpose, and creativity. That's when real momentum starts to build.

Every year, during the annual goal-setting process with my team, I make sure that there's always a personal growth goal included. We tie these personal growth goals to annual bonuses, so, in a way, we pay people to learn and grow. We do this more to encourage team members to expand their horizons, improve themselves, and bring more value not just to the company, but to their own lives.

Individuals may pursue self-improvement through learning, networking, or personal projects. A significant impact is created by empowering individuals to pursue their passions. The benefits are twofold. First, as humans, we're at our best when we are continuously learning. There's just more fulfillment in life when we're growing. Second, learning something new or brushing up on skills we've learned before sparks creativity. All of this is individually beneficial, which in turn, brings fresh energy to the entire team.

The surprising part is that about 50% of the new team members that join our company push back the first time we discuss personal growth goals. This concept is new to them. They haven't considered personal growth goals in a company goal setting. Honestly, this blows my mind. We're talking about a global business culture where leaders caring about their people growing is such a foreign idea that half of our new team members can't even think of a goal for themselves! After this initial goal setting, the concept proves more popular. They use it as an opportunity to take a class they've been eyeing, attend industry seminars, or get certified in something that sparks their interest.

I think part of my job as a leader is to help people not only figure out what those growth goals are but also help them achieve those goals. Whether it's guiding them towards an interesting course they can take, introducing them to a peer they can network with, or just giving them the time and space they need to work on a passion project, my goal is always to empower them to grow. Here are a few practical tips that have helped me set personal growth goals with my team:

Make Goals Relevant: Your personal growth goal should align with your business or industry. If you're in industrial automation, it makes little sense for someone to go out and get their real estate license (unless, of course, your company plans to invest in property). Keeping the goal relevant ensures it benefits both the individual and the company.

Utilize Continuous Learning Benefits: If your company offers continuous learning benefits, encourage your team to take advantage of them. Whether it's earning a certificate, attending a seminar, or taking part in a workshop, these benefits are there for a reason. This alignment of personal growth and company investment in its people is achieved by using these learning benefits.

Don't Always Focus on Weaknesses: Often, people default to wanting to work on their weaknesses when setting a growth goal. Unless a weakness is a glaring issue that needs immediate attention, I usually steer them away from that. Instead, let's focus on building strengths or exploring new opportunities within our industry. Forward-thinking goals are usually far more engaging and valuable in the long run. For instance, think about HR leaders before the COVID pandemic. How many of them would have loved to be certified in remote work models before COVID changed everything overnight?

Personal growth goals are a powerful tool, and as leaders, encouraging and supporting our teams in this journey is on us. More importantly than just creating better employees, when we make space for personal growth, we're helping create happier, more fulfilled people. And that's something everyone benefits from.

Creating a Lasting Legacy

Leading by example isn't just about driving performance today. It's about creating a lasting legacy that endures long after you're gone. A true legacy is the impact you make that carries forward, shaping not just the culture of your current team, but influencing future leaders who take the reins after you. Legacy isn't about being liked—because that's not always possible—but about leaving a legacy built on respect, integrity, and authenticity that is wildly achievable. When leaders consistently model values-driven behavior, they create a ripple effect that influences people and organizational culture far beyond their tenure.

Earlier, I shared how Rod left an indelible mark on my career. His commitment to authenticity and ethical leadership set the foundation for the type of leader I wanted to be. Now, let me introduce you to Joel, someone who consistently led by example and built an incredible team rooted in trust and collaboration. The first time I truly witnessed the power of leading by example was at my very first job—where Joel's leadership changed everything I thought I knew about culture and accountability.

These two individuals didn't just influence my thinking—they shaped the way I lead today. Their impact didn't end with them. It lives on through the choices I make and the example I try to set for others.

My Journey: My First Experience Witnessing Leading by Example

I had my first job right out of college at a roll-form steel company, where I took part in a management training program. The plant where I trained and worked had one of the best teams I have ever been a part of. It was an incredibly close-knit group that operated like a family. We spent the entire day at the plant, socialized during evenings and weekends, and consistently supported one another. Working long nights or weekends to help a department catch up or fix something that had gone wrong was not uncommon—and we had fun doing it. Our Plant Manager, Joel, was the driving force behind this unity. He instilled a "team first" attitude that kept us all motivated and working towards a common goal. During my time there, Joel built an incredible culture that led to our plant consistently ranking as the #1 production facility in the U.S.

Joel didn't just expect us to work well together—he clarified that anyone who wasn't interested in supporting the culture wouldn't be a good fit for the team. There were people who resisted the positive changes Joel was making, and while that didn't make them bad people, they clearly didn't fit into the culture he envisioned. He didn't shy away from making tough decisions to ensure we had the right people, with the right attitude, in the right roles. Here are some key actions Joel took to lead by example that had a significant impact on the plant's success:

Transparent Communication: Joel always led with transparency, ensuring that everyone on the team knew where we stood. He held regular meetings to keep us updated on the plant's performance, what challenges were ahead, and what goals we were striving for. By communicating openly, Joel built trust within the team. Everyone generally agreed, and we always knew if we were winning or losing. There were no surprises, and we felt a shared sense of accountability for the success or failure of our goals. This transparency helped us all understand what needed to be done and how our work directly affected the plant's overall success.

Commitment to Quality: Joel's commitment to quality was clear every day. He would inspect the production lines, work alongside us when quality issues arose, and show his dedication to continuous improvement. Joel didn't just bark orders from his office—he dug in and worked alongside us. This commitment to quality set a high standard for everyone else to follow. His dedication inspired the rest of us to take pride in our work and focus on improving quality in everything we did.

Ethical Behavior: Joel adhered to ethical behavior and always did what was right even if doing so wasn't the easiest choice. One thing that stood out to me was how Joel approached hiring. He often interviewed and hired convicted felons, believing that everyone deserves a second chance. Joel believed that as long as they had the right attitude and fit the organization's culture, they deserved a chance to earn a living and join a great team. This wasn't just about filling vacancies. Joel's hiring practices showed the team that mistakes are a part of life, but they don't define us if we're committed to learning and growing.

The team found this message impactful. It wasn't just lip service—it showed that Joel genuinely believed in giving people opportunities and set a tone of empathy and understanding throughout the plant. It taught us it's okay to make mistakes as long as you work hard, have the right attitude, and stay committed to the team.

Empowerment & Recognition: Joel believed in empowering his team and actively looked for opportunities to recognize our wins. He'd constantly encourage us to break production records or hit daily goals. These were small wins in the grand scheme of things, but Joel always took the time to celebrate them with us. When we met a production target or broke a record, he made sure the entire team knew and celebrated. That recognition, no matter how small, reinforced the culture of excellence and showed us that our hard work didn't go unnoticed.

Joel also empowered us by giving us autonomy. He trusted us to make decisions on the floor and run with our ideas. This sense of ownership motivated us to do our best work and drove us to excel. It wasn't just about doing the job—it was about making an impact, contributing to the team's success, and knowing that our contributions mattered.

The impact of Joel's leadership was transformational. Employee morale soared and turnover was low. Our plant consistently led in production rankings because every team member committed to our shared goals. Joel's "team first" approach prioritized teamwork and fostered plant-wide respect, accountability, and dedication.

Joel's commitment to leading by example left a lasting legacy—not just on the plant's success, but also on every single person who worked there, including me. His leadership style, rooted in transparency, quality, empowerment, and ethical behavior, is something I carry with me to this day. I hope that through my leadership, I can pass on the lessons I learned from Joel and create a culture that inspires others the way he inspired me.

A key aspect of a lasting legacy is realizing that your reputation follows you wherever you go. Most industries are, in reality, quite small. The relationships you form, the respect you earn (or lose), and the way you conduct yourself become part of your story. Think back to Michael Scott from *The Office* or Harry Dunne from *Dumb and Dumber*—their reputations precede them, and people know what they're about even before meeting them. So, ask yourself: What's the narrative you want people to tell about you? Your legacy is your reputation, and it's being written in real time, through every interaction, every decision, and every opportunity to lead by example.

Leaving a legacy of leadership means leaving behind more than just results. You're leaving behind a culture that others want to be part of built on respect, mutual trust, and a commitment to growth. If you consistently show integrity, if you make decisions with honesty, and if you genuinely care for your people and their development, that's what you will be remembered for. That's what people will carry forward, and what will shape how they lead others.

Imagine your team continuing to hold themselves accountable, striving for excellence, and treating each other with respect long after you've moved on. The most accurate measure of a lasting legacy is the positive change you start that then outlives your presence. As for me, my goal is for the values Rod and Joel instilled in me to continue shaping future leaders through the way I lead today.

Building a lasting legacy means consistently showing integrity, owning your mistakes, and supporting the growth of those around you. It's about making the hard decisions when it's necessary, not taking shortcuts, and leading in a way that others want to emulate. Legacies develop gradually, resulting from numerous choices and actions taken over an extended period. Your legacy is the narrative others tell about you. Make sure it's a story worth telling, that reflects your authenticity, your commitment to doing the right thing, and your desire to lead by example in every aspect of your life. That's the legacy that lasts.

Practical Steps for Leading by Example

To further solidify the concepts discussed, here are practical steps leaders can take to enhance their ability to lead by example:

1. **Reflect on Your Values:** Take the time to reflect on your core values and how they align with your actions. Identify any gaps and make a commitment to align your behavior with your values.

2. **Set Clear Expectations:** Clearly communicate your expectations for behavior and performance to your team. Ensure that these expectations align with the organization's values and are achievable.

3. **Be Visible and Accessible:** Be visible and accessible to your team. Engage with team members regularly and show that you value their input and contributions.

4. **Take Responsibility:** Take responsibility for your actions and decisions, especially in challenging situations. Demonstrate integrity and accountability by owning up to mistakes and taking steps to rectify them.

5. **Empower Your Team:** Empower your team to make decisions based on shared values. Provide the support and resources to help them succeed and encourage innovation and creativity.

6. **Recognize and Reward:** Recognize and reward behaviors that align with the organization's values. Reinforce the importance of these values by acknowledging and celebrating those who exemplify them.

Final Thoughts: The Future of Leading by Example

Leading by example is at the heart of authentic leadership. Live out your values every day and serve as a beacon of integrity and authenticity for others to follow. Throughout this chapter, we've explored the significance of modeling authentic behavior and how doing so transforms an organization's culture through trust, accountability, and shared success. Leading by example sets us up where the actions we take today create a legacy that shapes the organization's future, and creates a place where people feel empowered, valued, and inspired to grow.

As leaders, our actions speak louder than our words. Through our actions we influence, inspire, and leave a lasting legacy. This legacy isn't about being liked; it's about being respected for upholding your values with consistency, integrity, and authenticity. In every interaction, we reinforce these values and ensure that our reputation reflects the impact we want to have. As the influence of mentors like Joel and Rod has left an indelible mark on my leadership, I strive to pass these principles to future leaders through my own actions.

Looking to the future, the importance of leading by example will only continue to grow. The rapid pace of change, coupled with the complexity of the global business environment, demands leaders who can navigate uncertainty with both authenticity and integrity. Because of emerging trends like remote work and digital transformation, setting a positive example is more crucial than ever.

In a remote work environment, maintaining visibility and accessibility becomes even more critical. Leaders must find new ways to stay present and connected with their teams, ensuring that everyone feels aligned with the organization's values, even when physically apart. The responsibility for cultivating trust and openness falls on leaders who must make themselves approachable, offer clarity, and foster a culture of collaboration amidst an environment of separation.

Digital transformation, meanwhile, brings both opportunities and challenges. Technology makes communication and information sharing easier than ever, but it also raises concerns about privacy, ethics, and employee well-being. Leaders within companies that have not yet adopted the technology developing in this evolving digital transformation will soon be left behind. Tools like AI-driven hiring platforms and employee monitoring software can increase efficiency, but they also require leaders to be transparent about how these tools are used to ensure fairness and data protection. Though cloud-based collaboration platforms improve teamwork and accessibility, they can muddy work-life boundaries if not managed correctly. By openly discussing these realities and ensuring personal information is safe, leaders demonstrate ethical decision-making and set a tone of trust.

Finally, leading by example involves cultivating a culture that encourages and celebrates personal growth. Taking an interest in the personal development of each team member and helping them pursue their own growth goals creates a more fulfilled and engaged workforce that drives collective success.

Leading by example is paramount for authentic leadership. By embracing integrity, accountability, and a commitment to the growth of others, leaders create a culture of trust and excellence that drives organizational performance and personal fulfillment. Creating a lasting legacy that continues to uplift and inspire those who follow you is a perpetual journey built one step at a time as you lead by example. The rewards, in terms of stronger relationships, greater engagement, and sustainable success, are worth every effort.

7

Embracing Vulnerability

Hugh Jackman, well known for playing the tough and fierce Wolverine in the X-Men series, once shared a humorous story about his experience preparing for The Greatest Showman. Despite his musical background, he was deeply nervous about the choreography and practiced obsessively in his living room, trying to get every step right. His commitment was so intense, he joked that even the family dog had become startled by his stomping, spinning, and singing. This moment of vulnerability showed that even a seemingly invincible superhero has moments of self-doubt and nerves. The humor of Jackman startling his dog made his insecurity relatable, while his admission highlighted the courage it takes to embrace vulnerability and push through fear, even as an established actor.

Embracing vulnerability as a component of authentic leadership is not about showcasing weaknesses, but about opening up to genuine connections, learning, and growth. Stepping away from the facade of infallibility in order to engage with others in a more authentic way takes courage. Vulnerability enables leaders to foster deeper relationships, build trust, and create an environment where everyone feels valued and empowered to contribute.

Like Hugh Jackman stepping out of his comfort zone, leaders must summon the courage to embrace vulnerability. As Brené Brown, a leading researcher on vulnerability, emphasizes that vulnerability is not a weakness—it's the birthplace of courage, innovation, and connection. Her groundbreaking studies provide a framework for understanding why vulnerability is a critical strength in leadership (Brown, 2018).

The Strength of Vulnerability in Leadership

You might think that showing vulnerability as a leader is risky. What if others perceive weakness or incompetence? While vulnerability may seem like a threat to your authority, it's actually one of the strongest assets you can bring to your leadership style. By embracing vulnerability, you invite authenticity into your workplace, and that authenticity is what will ultimately connect you with your team and build genuine respect.

Let's be real—being vulnerable can feel threatening, especially when you've worked so hard to establish your authority. You might wonder if admitting that you don't know the answer makes you look weak. The answer is no. True authority doesn't come from having all the answers but from being real, open, and willing to collaborate with others. Respect the structure and responsibilities of your role, but remember that being authentic will lead to greater long-term success than simply falling in line with rigid expectations of what authority should look like.

My Journey Into Vulnerability

In the early years of my career in the automation industry, I was driven by the pursuit of success in terms of promotions, accolades, and financial rewards. Fresh out of business school with an MBA, I landed a coveted project manager role at a fast-growing, family-owned automation company. Determined to prove myself, I worked tirelessly, often sacrificing my personal life. Within a year, I climbed the corporate ladder to a management position.

The higher I climbed, the more isolated I felt. My leadership style was authoritative, focused on proving my worth to company leadership rather than connecting with my team. I believed that showing vulnerability would prevent me from advancing. My approach, however, only made things worse. Turnover increased as my team grew disengaged and unmotivated.

A pivotal project finally forced me to confront my leadership style. The project required us to develop a new and innovative software solution under an incredibly tight deadline. As the pressure mounted, it became clear we were falling behind. As the project neared the brink of failure, I tried to micromanage every detail, but my team was unresponsive.

Desperate, I called an impromptu team meeting. For the first time, I opened up, admitting I didn't have all the answers. I shared my fears about the project's potential failure and how the pressure was affecting me personally. To my surprise, my team responded with empathy and support, sharing their own concerns and frustrations which I hadn't been aware of.

That moment of vulnerability broke down the barriers between us. We brainstormed solutions together, and I encouraged everyone to take ownership of their tasks. By involving my team in decision-making and valuing their input, we turned the project around and ultimately met our deadline and achieved a successful launch. My favorite memory from the project, post impromptu meeting, was the project team eating tacos together, in a circle, over a trashcan, at 2:00am, during a deploy at the customer's site. We were bitching, whining, laughing, and inhaling tacos as fast as we could so we could get back to work. That moment of comradery and unity is the memory that drove me to write this book.

This experience taught me that leadership isn't about having all the answers. It's about creating an environment where everyone feels valued and empowered. Because I embraced vulnerability, I connected with my team on a deeper level which built trust and collaboration. I realized that authentic leadership means being open about your challenges, which encourages others to do the same.

In the years since, I've attempted to lead with empathy and transparency. I seek regular feedback and prioritize understanding the unique strengths and aspirations of each team member. This shift has led to higher engagement, lower turnover, and a more innovative, resilient team. Because I embraced vulnerability, my leadership style transformed from one of authority to one of authenticity.

In contemporary leadership models, vulnerability plays an essential role. We no longer have command-and-control leadership styles that expect leaders to be infallible. Today, successful leadership centers around fostering collaboration, innovation, and emotional intelligence. In models such as transformational and servant leadership, vulnerability is not just encouraged, it's required. Transformational leaders inspire their teams by sharing their vision and personal stories, which often include setbacks and lessons learned. This openness makes their message more powerful and motivates their team to buy into the collective mission. Similarly, servant leaders focus on the growth and well-being of their teams, which also requires a willingness to share personal challenges and be open about what they don't know.

As Brené Brown highlights in her TEDx Houston talk that has been viewed over 60 million times, vulnerability is "uncertainty, risk, and emotional exposure" and it is the foundation of courageous leadership. By sharing personal experiences or lessons learned from setbacks, leaders inspire their teams to take similar risks and foster creativity and innovation. For example, a manager admitting, "I don't have the answer right now, but let's figure it out together," creates a collaborative atmosphere where everyone feels empowered to contribute (Brown, 2010).

Here are a few tips on how to be vulnerable without feeling like you're losing your authority:

---

1. **Start Small:** You don't have to share your biggest fears or failures on day one. Begin with smaller steps. Acknowledge when you've made a mistake or admit when you're unsure about something. This will gradually build your comfort with being vulnerable and show your team that it's okay to do the same.

---

2. **Be Intentional:** Vulnerability is about sharing with a purpose, not over sharing. Ask yourself, "Will sharing this help my team?" If the answer is yes—whether it's helping them learn from your experience or encouraging them to be open—then it's worth sharing.

---

3. **Balance vulnerability with confidence:** Vulnerability is powerful, but it's also important to balance it with confidence. Ensure your team understands that you're committed to collaboratively finding solutions, even if you don't currently possess all the answers. This balance will strengthen your authority and foster trust.

---

4. **Focus on Authenticity:** Remember, the goal is not to put on a performance, but to be authentic. When you share your experiences, do so because you genuinely want to connect and grow, not because you think it's what others expect. Authenticity always reveals itself.

Vulnerability is not about shedding all authority. You actually enhance authority through connection, empathy, and openness. Just like Hugh Jackman stepped out of his comfort zone to learn how to dance, you have to step out of yours to embrace vulnerability in your leadership. You might feel uncomfortable at first, but the connections you'll make and the respect you'll earn are worth the effort.

Contemporary leadership models recognize that vulnerability is an asset, not a liability. It brings humanity into the workplace, which builds resilience, creativity, and trust. When you lead with vulnerability, you're not just guiding your team—you're inviting them to come on the journey with you, to learn, to fail, to grow, and to succeed together. That's where the genuine power lies in leadership today.

Vulnerability as a Catalyst for Connection

Building trust through vulnerability is not just an abstract ideal—it's a measurable reality. Brené Brown's insights into vulnerability are supported by Google's *Project Aristotle*, an extensive study examining what factors distinguish effective teams. After analyzing 180 teams, the research revealed that psychological safety—a collective belief that the group is a secure space for interpersonal risk-taking—was the single most important element for high-performing teams. Teams characterized by high psychological safety saw 50% higher productivity, 76% greater engagement, and 27% lower turnover compared to others (Pretty, 2024). How do you build a psychologically safe environment? Vulnerability.

Leaders who openly embraced vulnerability by acknowledging mistakes or uncertainties created environments in which team members felt empowered to take risks and freely contribute ideas. These findings underscore that vulnerability is not just a personal virtue but also a powerful driver of organizational success. By modeling vulnerability, leaders initiate a ripple effect that enhances psychological safety which cultivates deeper, more meaningful connections within their teams.

Additionally, shared vulnerability significantly enhances team cohesion by encouraging a sense of unity and collective purpose. When team members observe their leaders demonstrating vulnerability, they feel inspired and safer to open up about their own experiences. This mutual openness not only strengthens interpersonal bonds but also builds genuine camaraderie, substantially boosting team effectiveness.

Finally, embracing vulnerability promotes an environment of psychological safety where individuals can freely express ideas, voice concerns, and admit errors without fear of repercussions. Such an environment is essential for fostering innovation and creativity, as team members become comfortable exploring bold, new ideas without the fear of failure or harsh criticism. In short, vulnerability not only deepens personal connections—it actively creates the foundation necessary for organizational growth, innovation, and lasting success.

Overcome the Fear of Vulnerability: Strategies for Authentic Leaders

Re-enter Hugh Jackman. People view him as having incredible authority on screen. After all, Wolverine isn't exactly a character who shows a lot of self-doubt. But when Jackman shared his fear of dancing and the struggles he faced during rehearsals, people connected with him on a deeper level. Many of us can relate to feeling out of our element sometimes. That vulnerability didn't make Jackman less of a superhero but made him more relatable, and ultimately more respected. You can apply the same principles in your own leadership. By showing that you also have areas where you're learning, you invite your team to see you as someone who is growing alongside them.

So how do you actually begin to embrace vulnerability as a leader? Start by addressing the fear head-on and building the habit, step by step.

Here are a few strategies to help you develop the confidence and clarity to lead with vulnerability and to make it one of your greatest strengths:

Confront Fear Head-On: Fear of judgment, weakness, and exploitation often block the path to embracing vulnerability. Overcoming these fears requires a shift in perspective from viewing vulnerability as a liability to seeing it as an asset to leadership and team development. The key is understanding that vulnerability is actually a sign of strength, and demonstrates the courage to be open and authentic, even in the face of uncertainty.

Self-Reflection and Awareness: To overcome the fear of vulnerability, we must start with self-reflection. Think about what makes you hesitant to be open. Ask yourself: What am I afraid of? How might these fears be holding me back as a leader? This self-awareness helps you recognize how your fears may be affecting your behavior and relationships. Techniques like journaling, meditation, and seeking feedback from trusted colleagues can help you better understand the barriers to being vulnerable.

Gradual Exposure: Becoming comfortable with vulnerability requires practice and gradual exposure. Take a step-by-step approach, starting with small disclosures and gradually increasing openness as trust within the team strengthens. This incremental approach helps you build confidence and allows you to observe the positive effects of vulnerability on team dynamics and trust.

For example, start by sharing a minor mistake you made and what you learned from it. As you become more comfortable, you can share more significant challenges or experiences. This kind of gradual exposure not only helps you get used to being vulnerable but also shows to your team that it's safe to take risks and open up.

Fostering a Supportive Culture: Cultivating an organizational culture that values and supports vulnerability is essential for creating an environment where everyone feels safe to open up. Leaders play a crucial role in setting the tone by modeling vulnerability themselves—sharing challenges, admitting mistakes, and seeking feedback. This openness encourages team members to follow suit. Intentionally creating opportunities for open dialogue, including regular team check-ins, dedicated reflection sessions, or casual conversations, reinforces a culture of safety. Establishing clear guidelines around respect and empathy ensures we value all contributions, further encouraging team members to express themselves without fear of judgment. When leaders foster such a supportive culture, they pave the way for trust, collaboration, and authentic engagement across the organization.

The Ripple Effect of Vulnerable Leadership

The impact of vulnerable leadership extends far beyond individual leaders or even their immediate teams. When leaders choose to lead with authenticity and openness, they create a ripple effect that transforms the organizational culture, enhances collaboration, and even strengthens external relationships.

The core of this ripple effect is the trust and psychological safety fostered by vulnerability. When leaders model vulnerability by admitting mistakes, seeking feedback, or openly sharing challenges, they send a powerful message to their teams that it's okay to be human. This openness breaks down barriers, empowering team members to take risks, share bold ideas, and engage in honest dialogue without fear of judgment.

Consider a leader who openly discusses a significant failure in a company-wide meeting in order to highlight the lessons learned instead of dwelling on the setbacks. That single act of vulnerability can encourage others to reframe their mistakes as opportunities for growth rather than moments of shame. Over time, this mindset permeates the organization and creates a culture where continuous improvement and innovation thrive.

The effect of vulnerability doesn't stop at internal dynamics. It also transforms external relationships with clients, partners, and stakeholders. When organizations adopt a transparent and open approach, they build stronger trust and loyalty with those they serve. Vulnerability humanizes the organization, showing that it values integrity and connection to perfection.

One of the most interesting aspects of this ripple effect is how it inspires future leaders. Vulnerability, when modeled by senior leaders, gives emerging leaders the confidence to lead authentically. It embeds itself into the DNA of the organization and creates a legacy of openness and resilience that outlasts any one leader.

Imagine an organization where vulnerability cascades at every level—from senior executives to front-line employees. Teams collaborate freely. The organization celebrates innovation and treats failures as steppingstones.

Such an environment is not only more productive, but also more meaningful for everyone involved. This is the lasting power of vulnerable leadership. Vulnerability transforms organizations into places where people can thrive together.

By embracing vulnerability, leaders set off a chain reaction of trust, connection, and growth that ripples outward, strengthening both the people and the organizations they serve.

Transforming Organizational Culture

When vulnerability becomes part of the leadership equation, it can transform the entire organizational culture into one that values honesty, transparency, and openness. This sets the tone that everyone—no matter their position—can bring their full selves to work. This kind of openness helps dismantle those traditional barriers that often stifle communication and replaces them with trust and collaboration.

My Journey: The Impact of Vulnerable Leadership

To illustrate the impact of vulnerable leadership, let me share a story about a tech company that went through a remarkable cultural transformation—all thanks to a new CEO who led with vulnerability. When this CEO came in, the company was struggling. Employee morale was low, turnover was high, and innovation was practically nonexistent. Something had to change, and this new leader realized that the key to turning things around wasn't just about strategy—it was about connection.

The first thing the CEO did was embrace open communication. She held regular town hall meetings where anyone could ask questions or share concerns. No topics were off-limits. During these meetings, the CEO openly talked about the company's challenges and admitted that she didn't have all the answers. It wasn't easy, but this honesty started building a culture of transparency and trust. People felt like they were really part of the conversation, not just cogs in a machine.

The next step was to encourage experimentation. The CEO clearly communicated to the team that experimentation, including potential failures, was acceptable. They reframed mistakes as learning opportunities, sparking creativity with this alternative approach. Suddenly, people weren't afraid to think innovatively or suggest that wild idea they'd been holding back. Failure wasn't a scary word anymore; it was just part of the journey.

The focus then extended beyond the company's challenges as the CEO shared her own personal experiences. She shared stories of her own struggles as she was building her career and the lessons she learned from failures along the way. This kind of openness was contagious. Team members reflected on their own experiences and felt inspired to grow. Openness became the norm, strengthening trust and connection throughout the team.

The CEO also put effort into fostering a supportive culture. She made space for people to share their experiences, not just in formal meetings, but also in casual settings. She even created a recognition program to celebrate those who showed vulnerability—people who were brave enough to speak up about their challenges or take risks despite uncertainty. These actions changed the company's DNA.

The results were truly amazing. Employee morale improved. A stronger sense of community and purpose developed amongst employees. Turnover rates dropped, and innovation flourished again. The company's culture became one where transparency, support, and openness were the new normal. The CEO's commitment to embracing vulnerability created a lasting legacy that transformed the company's culture and set the stage for long-term success

Encouraging Innovation and Learning

A culture that values vulnerability also paves the way for greater innovation and learning. As a leader, when you model vulnerability, you help create an environment where taking risks, sharing unconventional ideas, and challenging norms becomes part of the culture. When people feel safe from judgment or punitive repercussions, they're much more inclined to push boundaries, innovate, and explore what's possible.

In this kind of environment, failure is part of the journey, not a dead-end. Vulnerable leaders believe that mistakes are natural steppingstones for growth. Instead of focusing on blame, they encourage their teams to examine what went wrong, what worked, and how to do better next time. This approach turns setbacks into valuable learning moments and drives a culture of continuous improvement.

A leader who actively encourages their team to try fresh approaches, even if there's a risk of failure, sends a simple message: innovation matters more than perfection. Team members feel empowered to experiment, knowing that even if things don't go as planned, it's an opportunity to learn and grow. This acceptance of failure leads to more creativity, as people become more willing to test new ideas, iterate, and build on one another's contributions. The outcome? A resilient, innovative team that's equipped to tackle challenges head-on, without fear.

Enhance Personal Growth and Development

Vulnerability also plays a big role in personal growth and development. When leaders model vulnerability, they send a powerful message that self-awareness and growth are never-ending journeys. By openly talking about their own challenges, setbacks, and lessons learned, leaders show their teams that it's okay to not have everything figured out all the time. This approach helps normalize learning through mistakes and makes growth a shared experience rather than an isolated struggle.

For instance, imagine a leader who shares their story about overcoming a significant setback in their career. By doing this, they inspire their team members to reflect on their own experiences and find areas for growth. Sharing personal struggles like that creates a safe space where people feel comfortable acknowledging their weaknesses and pursuing self-improvement without fear of judgment.

Vulnerability, when embraced as part of the culture, fosters a more engaged and motivated workforce. Team members are not only encouraged to grow but also feel supported in that growth. This focus on personal development builds a growth mindset, empowering individuals to reach their full potential while staying motivated and resilient. A focus on both individual and collective growth within an organization sets the stage for team-wide success.

Practical Steps for Embracing Vulnerability

Embracing vulnerability, especially when in a leadership role, can feel daunting. But the benefits of leading with authenticity, fostering connection, and creating an atmosphere where innovation thrives are undeniable. To help make vulnerability a more approachable and practical part of your leadership style, here are some concrete steps to guide you along the way:

Engage in Self-Reflection: The journey to vulnerability begins with understanding yourself. Explore your fears and resistance to vulnerability. What makes you hesitant to open up? Self-reflection is about getting comfortable with your insecurities and acknowledging the things that make you uncomfortable. Techniques like journaling, meditation, and seeking feedback from trusted colleagues can help you gain insights into your behavior and mindset. For example, journaling lets you express your thoughts freely, unburdened by judgment, while meditation fosters grounding and clarity. Seeking feedback is also powerful—sometimes others can see the barriers we put up more clearly than we can ourselves. Being open to hearing about these barriers is one of the first steps toward breaking them down.

Commit to Baby Steps: Vulnerability doesn't mean you need to start by disclosing everything you've ever done wrong or that scares you. Begin with something small. Perhaps admit a minor mistake you made or share a minor challenge you're facing. By doing this, you build a bridge of openness and trust with your team. The idea is to ease into vulnerability at your own pace, allowing yourself to become comfortable with the process. As you practice this, you'll find it easier to share more significant challenges and even welcome others to do the same. By starting small, you're creating opportunities for your team to share their experiences, too.

Model Vulnerability: As a leader, your actions set the tone for your organization. If you want your team to embrace vulnerability, you need to model it yourself. Talk openly about challenges you've faced, uncertainties you have, or mistakes you've made. When your team sees you being authentic, they'll feel encouraged to follow suit. Modeling vulnerability doesn't mean over sharing or constantly highlighting negative experiences; it's about showing your human side. This builds credibility and shows that everyone, regardless of their position, has struggles and areas where they're still learning. Creating safe spaces for open dialogue is key to fostering a team environment where members feel comfortable expressing themselves. It could be something as simple as adding the question "What's one thing you struggled with this week" to your regular meetings. Your willingness to model this behavior will pave the way for others to share openly.

Create an Atmosphere of Trust: Vulnerability flourishes in an environment where it is valued and supported. Build an organizational culture that accepts and celebrates openness. This means encouraging dialogue and building an atmosphere of trust. Team members should regularly share their experiences through check-ins, reflective sessions, or informal get-togethers. It's important to make sure your team knows that it's safe to express their concerns without fear of judgment or repercussions. Celebrate the moments when someone takes a risk, admits they don't have all the answers, or shows their human side. You might even establish norms that support these behaviors, such as openly discussing what went wrong in a project without blame or judgment. Fostering a supportive culture takes time and consistency, but the payoff is enormous—a team that trusts each other deeply and feels safe enough to bring their best, most authentic selves to work every day.

Embrace Failure as Learning: One of the most significant barriers to vulnerability is the fear of failure. As a leader, you have the power to shift the perspective on failure by viewing it as a natural part of the learning process as opposed to seeing it as a setback. Promote the idea that mistakes are an opportunity to grow, not something to fear. This means not only saying that failure is acceptable but showing it in your actions. If a project doesn't go as planned, don't sweep your frustrations under the rug—talk openly about what went wrong. Discuss what worked, what didn't, and what you can learn from everything as a team. Make these conversations positive and focused on improvement rather than blame. Your team will feel more comfortable taking risks and innovating when they see you using failure as a building block for future success instead of something to be punished for. This approach fosters creativity, resilience, and continuous growth. Remember, vulnerability isn't just about being open when things are going well—it's about how you handle setbacks, showing that mistakes are a part of the journey, not the end.

Seek and Encourage Feedback: Being vulnerable also means being open to feedback whether it's good or bad. Cultivate a culture where people welcome feedback as a tool for growth. Ask your team for their input on your leadership and be willing to take their insights to heart. Not only does this show your willingness to grow, but it also shows that you value your team's perspectives. When you openly seek feedback, you're not only embracing vulnerability, but you're also giving your team permission to do the same. This will encourage them to use feedback, fostering continuous improvement and mutual support.

Be Present and Listen: Part of embracing vulnerability is showing up fully for your team. This means practicing active listening and being present during conversations. When someone is sharing their thoughts or challenges, give them your full attention. This signals that you genuinely care about their experience, which builds trust and a culture of openness. Vulnerability involves acknowledging uncertainty and embracing diverse perspectives. Sometimes, just being present and listening is one of the most vulnerable acts you can perform as it shows you don't always need to be the solution provider.

By following these steps, you'll create a work environment where vulnerability is not only acceptable but is a core strength of your leadership style. The benefits will ripple through your organization, leading to stronger connections, greater innovation, and a resilient culture where everyone feels empowered to contribute authentically. Vulnerability takes courage and the transformation it brings to both personal and team dynamics is undeniably worth the effort.

Final Thoughts: The Future of Vulnerable Leadership

People often misunderstand vulnerability as a weakness, but, as this chapter has explored, it is one of the greatest strengths a leader can embody. Admitting when you don't have all the answers, seeking feedback, and openly sharing challenges takes courage. By doing so, leaders pave the way for connection, trust, and growth both for themselves and for their teams.

When leaders embrace vulnerability, they foster an environment where people feel safe to share ideas, admit mistakes, and take risks. This psychological safety unlocks creativity and innovation, creating a culture where continuous improvement becomes second nature. Vulnerable leadership also builds resilience by encouraging teams to view challenges and setbacks as opportunities for learning, rather than moments of failure.

But the impact doesn't stop within the organization. Vulnerability humanizes leaders, making them more relatable and authentic in their relationships with clients, partners, and stakeholders. It shows that leadership isn't about perfection but about integrity, connection, and the willingness to grow alongside those you lead.

As you reflect on the concepts in this chapter, consider how vulnerability can shape your own leadership journey. Start small, share intentionally, and focus on authenticity. Each act of vulnerability sets off a ripple effect, inspiring others to do the same and building a culture of trust, innovation, and collaboration.

In a world that often values certainty and control, choosing vulnerability is a radical act. Choosing to lead with courage, to connect on a deeper level, and to inspire those around you to bring their entire selves to the table is a choice you make. Embracing vulnerability isn't just about being a better leader; it's about creating a more human, resilient, and innovative organization. The ripple effects of your choice to lead with vulnerability will not only transform your teams but will also leave a lasting legacy of trust and growth.

8

Nurturing Empathy and Inclusivity

What do the best leaders have in common? It's not just strategy, vision, or charisma—it's the ability to connect on a deeply human level. Empathy and inclusivity build thriving teams. When people feel truly seen, heard, and valued, instead of just showing up to do the job, they bring the best version of themselves to work.

Imagine this: A team member has been missing deadlines and seems disengaged. Jumping to conclusions or issuing a warning would be easy. Now, picture a leader pausing and asking the simple question of "Is everything okay?" Because you have already created a safe space for honesty, someone who is struggling is more likely to expound on what is actually going on, as opposed to projecting on someone or something else, or responding with the perfunctory "I'm fine." That one moment of genuine concern could reveal something deeper like family stress, health challenges, or burnout. By leaning into empathy, the leader turns a potential conflict into an opportunity for trust and support.

What does it mean to truly lead with empathy and inclusivity? It's more than just showing kindness or supporting diversity. It's about creating an environment where people feel psychologically safe to be themselves. Empathy connects us to the heartbeat of our teams, while inclusivity ensures that every voice contributes to the rhythm.

In this chapter, we'll explore the practical ways leaders can nurture these traits. You'll discover how small shifts in perspective can unlock creative potential and how supporting diverse voices can elevate team performance. Empathy and inclusivity are moral imperatives and strategic advantages that drive innovation, resilience, and loyalty.

As you read on, consider your own leadership journey. How often do you check in on your team—not just their output, but their well-being? Do you foster environments that welcome every idea, and listen to every voice? Let's dive into how empathy and inclusivity can transform not only your leadership style but also the culture and success of your organization.

The Power and Practice of Empathy in Leadership

Empathy is more than a leadership buzzword—it's the ability to understand and value your team members as individuals and to see beyond their roles to recognize their unique challenges, perspectives, and contributions. True empathy creates trust, fosters collaboration, and cultivates a sense of belonging that drives performance and innovation.

Empathy begins with connection. Think about the last time someone truly listened to you—not just nodded along, but gave you their full attention, asked thoughtful questions, and made you feel understood. That moment likely strengthened your trust in them and left you feeling valued. Now imagine bringing that same transformative attentiveness to your leadership interactions.

Empathy is being present and creating space for open, honest dialog, not necessarily about having all the answers or trying to fix every problem. When leaders genuinely listen without judgment and validate emotions, they build bridges of trust that make sharing thoughts and ideas easier for team members. This fosters an environment where psychological safety thrives, empowering people to take risks, voice concerns, and contribute authentically.

Take the hypothetical story of James and Sara. James, a customer support manager, was struggling to meet deadlines while juggling the demands of a new baby at home. His performance slipped, targets were missed, his response times were slower, and he had declining energy. Sara, his leader, could have focused solely on the metrics and issued a warning. Instead, she noticed the change and started a conversation.

"James, I've noticed you've been a bit off lately," Sara began. "You're such a big part of this team, and I want to make sure you're okay. Is there anything I can do to support you right now?"

That single empathetic question opened the door to an honest dialogue. James shared he had struggles in his personal life that were affecting his ability to focus at work. Together, they devised a temporary plan to adjust his workload while ensuring the team can still meet its goals. This moment of empathy solved a performance issue and, even more importantly, deepened trust, renewed James's focus, and reinforced the team's sense of mutual support.

When leaders lead with empathy, they create a ripple effect that extends beyond individual interactions and into the team environment. Teams with empathetic leaders are more engaged, collaborative, and innovative. Employees feel valued not just for their output but for who they are, which drives loyalty and fosters a culture of mutual respect.

Empathy is a skill that grows with practice. Leaders can cultivate empathy by focusing fully on their team members during conversations, asking open-ended questions, and restating what they hear to ensure understanding. Regular check-ins with simple questions like, "How are you feeling about your workload?" or "Is there anything I can support you with today?" followed by actionable behavior, demonstrate care and build rapport. Showing understanding involves acknowledging emotions without judgment even if the situation can't be fixed.

Empathy without intention is an empty gesture. By showing up with genuine care and making small, consistent efforts, leaders build deeper connections, foster trust, and create environments where both people and innovation thrive. The power and practice of empathy is a leadership skill that transforms teams and inspires excellence.

One of the most interesting examples of empathy-driven leadership transforming an organization is Satya Nadella's leadership at Microsoft. When Nadella took over as CEO in 2014, Microsoft had a toxic, highly competitive culture that stifled collaboration and innovation. Instead of enforcing stricter policies, he focused on building a culture of empathy and inclusivity.

Nadella shifted Microsoft's culture by encouraging employees to see challenges as opportunities for growth rather than obstacles to overcome. He invested in leadership training focused on listening and understanding and created a culture where psychological safety became a priority.

The results were significant. Microsoft's market valuation eventually rose from around $300 billion to over $1 trillion, and employee satisfaction reached new highs (Nadella et al., 2018). By emphasizing empathy as a strategic leadership tool, Nadella transformed not only the company's culture but also its business success.

Emotional Intelligence Development

Emotional intelligence (EQ) is another critical aspect of empathetic leadership. It involves being aware of both your own emotions and those of others and using that awareness to guide your interactions effectively. Here are some ways to strengthen your emotional intelligence:

Self-Awareness: Self-awareness sits at the core of emotional intelligence. Before you can understand others' emotions, you need to understand your own emotions, what triggers them, and how they affect your thoughts and behaviors. Regular self-reflection is key. Try setting aside time each day to think about how you reacted to different situations. Journaling is a helpful tool here because it lets you record and process your feelings. Seeking feedback from trusted colleagues provides an external perspective that can help you see blind spots in your behavior.

Self-Regulation: Self-regulation is about managing your emotions effectively, especially in stressful situations. It's easy to be empathetic when things are going smoothly, but doing so is much more challenging when emotions are running high. Learning techniques like deep breathing, meditation, or even taking a moment to step away can help keep your emotions in check. By staying composed, you model calm and thoughtful behavior for your team, which makes doing the same easier for them.

Empathy in Practice: Cultivating empathy involves deliberately putting yourself in others' shoes in order to understand and relate to what someone else is feeling. One effective way to build empathy is through role-playing exercises where you imagine yourself in someone else's position. Another idea is to attend empathy workshops that guide leaders through exercises designed to enhance their ability to understand others' perspectives. The more you practice empathy, the more naturally it comes in real-life interactions.

Making Empathy a Leadership Habit: To truly cultivate empathy, leaders need to incorporate being empathetic as a daily practice rather than an occasional effort. This means embedding empathy in all your actions, no matter how small. It's not just about the big decisions; it's also in the day-to-day interactions—how you greet someone in the hallway, how you respond when someone is clearly having a tough day, and how you encourage dialogue even in casual conversations.

Another important aspect is modeling empathy for your team. When leaders are openly empathetic empathy becomes part of the team culture, encouraging everyone to support each other. This is important in high-pressure environments where stress can lead to misunderstanding and conflict.

Last, empathy is about showing up with genuine concern and trying your best. Employees don't expect leaders to have all the answers, but they appreciate leaders who will listen, acknowledge challenges, and support them through difficult times. Empathy is about striving to understand, and even if you don't always get it right, the effort alone can mean a lot to your team.

Empathy is not just a feel-good concept; it fosters the trust and connection in any team or organization. When leaders consistently show empathy, they create an environment where psychological safety flourishes, enabling team members to take risks, share ideas, and innovate. But the impact of empathy doesn't stop at individual relationships. It sets the stage for something even more transformative: inclusivity.

Why Inclusive Organizations Make Sense

Inclusivity builds on what empathy provides, ensuring that every individual not only feels heard but also can contribute meaningfully. This isn't just about creating a harmonious workplace—it's about leveraging the diverse perspectives of a team to drive innovation, collaboration, and long-term success.

While being inclusive is the right thing to do, it also improves employee performance. Research consistently shows that diverse and inclusive organizations outperform their counterparts. A 2020 McKinsey study found that companies in the top quartile for gender and ethnic diversity were 35% more likely to outperform their industry peers (Hunt, V. et al., 2020). Why? Diverse teams drive innovation, improve decision-making, and enhance problem-solving. Organizations that prioritize inclusivity also develop greater adaptability and resilience which are essential qualities in today's rapidly changing business landscape.

Now think about diversity and inclusivity. Picture a brainstorming session where everyone at the table comes from similar backgrounds and perspectives. Ideas flow, but they follow the same well-worn paths. Now imagine a team with diverse experiences—different cultures, identities, and viewpoints. Suddenly, the conversation is alive with fresh ideas and innovative solutions. Inclusivity's transformative power ensures that every voice has a seat at the table and every perspective receives value.

Inclusivity also enhances organizational resilience. Teams that not only value diverse perspectives but include those voices in every aspect are better equipped to navigate complexity and uncertainty. By actively seeking input from a range of voices, leaders can expect challenges more effectively and develop well-rounded solutions. Consider a company designing a global product—those who incorporate cultural insights from employees across different regions won't just avoid missteps; they'll create a product that resonates with a broader audience and captures new market opportunities.

Making Inclusivity an Everyday Leadership Practice

Creating an inclusive organization requires intention and demands action. Leaders play a critical role in shaping an environment where every voice is heard and valued.

A good leadership team that wants to embrace inclusivity in everyday practice can incorporate the following:

1. Rotate leadership roles in meetings so that quieter team members or those from underrepresented groups have opportunities to contribute from leadership positions.
2. Encourage quieter team members and those from underrepresented groups to share their input to ensure diverse perspectives inform decision-making.
3. Implement mentorship programs to empower underrepresented employees by providing career development and leadership opportunities.

Inclusivity thrives when reinforced through small, consistent actions. Acknowledging team members' contributions—thanking someone for a fresh perspective or highlighting a creative idea helps build a culture of appreciation. Leaders can also challenge biases in decision-making, whether through blind hiring practices or actively soliciting diverse viewpoints in key discussions. These deliberate efforts promote fairness and strengthen innovation, trust, and performance.

Debunking the Myth: Inclusivity Slows Organizations Down

Some leaders hesitate to prioritize inclusivity because they believe it slows decision-making or disrupts team cohesion. However, research disproves this concern. Studies by McKinsey and BCG show that companies with diverse leadership teams consistently outperform their competitors, not just in profitability, but in adaptability and innovation (Lorenzo, R. et al., 2018). Far from being a burden, including diverse perspectives speeds up problem-solving, enhances collaboration, and drives long-term resilience.

Inclusive organizations don't just perform better. They inspire trust and loyalty among employees and the communities they serve. When leaders prioritize inclusivity, they create workplaces where people feel valued, empowered, and motivated to bring their best selves to work. This is one of the smartest investment an organization can make. By embracing inclusivity as a strategic imperative, leaders unlock their teams' full potential, driving meaningful and sustainable success.

A Natural Outcome, Not a Forced Metric

We cannot reduce inclusivity to quotas or forced metrics. While some may see these as tangible indicators of progress, relying on them alone undermines the authenticity of true inclusion. Inclusivity isn't about meeting a numerical target. It's about creating a culture where diversity thrives because people feel included, valued and empowered to contribute.

While inclusivity is essential, many well-intentioned leaders struggle with unconscious bias, even when they believe they're making fair decisions. Harvard's Joan C. Williams shows that companies can fight unconscious bias by structurally changing their organization, not just by setting quotas (Williams, 2021).

Some effective "bias interrupters" leaders can implement include:

Blind hiring practices: Removing names and demographic details from resumes, candidates are evaluated based solely on skills and experience.

Structured decision-making: Using clear, objective criteria for promotions and performance evaluations rather than relying on gut instinct.

These small but strategic shifts actively promote inclusivity as a daily practice, ensuring that all voices are genuinely valued and not merely represented. Organizations that tout diversity for the sake of saying they are diverse and inclusive instead of actually valuing diversity and inclusivity undermine trust both within the organization and among the very individuals these metrics aim to include. Instead, leaders must anchor their actions in their moral compass, ensuring that their approach to empathy and inclusivity is driven by genuine care and commitment, not external pressures.

When leaders focus on fostering environments built on trust, empathy, and shared values, inclusivity becomes a natural byproduct. It's not about fulfilling quotas but about ensuring that every individual feels empowered to show up as his or her authentic self and contribute fully. Inclusivity built on these principles meets and exceeds expectations by creating lasting cultural transformation.

Metrics can be valuable tools for assessing progress and identifying areas of improvement. However, they must always serve as a reflection of deeper, values-driven efforts and not as a substitute for them. Leaders should ask themselves if they are pursuing something because it aligns with their values, or because it satisfies external expectations. The answer to that question should always tie back to your moral compass.

Inclusivity flourishes when it's rooted in empathy and integrity. By rejecting performative metrics and staying true to your core values, you can build organizations where inclusivity is celebrated as a source of strength and innovation.

Inclusive Policies and Practices

Developing and implementing policies and practices that support inclusivity is essential for creating a supportive work environment.

Flexible Working Arrangements: Offering flexible working arrangements can accommodate the diverse needs of employees, including remote work options, flexible hours, and parental leave.

Equitable Opportunity Structures: Ensure that all employees have access to the same opportunities for advancement, training, and development, regardless of their background or identity.

Anti-Discrimination Measures: Implement and enforce policies that prevent discrimination and harassment, creating a safe and respectful workplace for everyone.

Cultivating a Culture of Belonging

Creating a culture where everyone feels they belong and can thrive involves ongoing efforts to celebrate diversity and promote inclusivity.

Bias Training and Inclusivity Workshops: Regularly scheduled training on unconscious bias and inclusive behaviors will raise awareness and promote inclusivity.

Team-Building Activities: Organize team-building activities that celebrate diversity and encourage collaboration and understanding among team members.

Employee Resource Groups: Support the formation of employee resource groups (ERGs) that provide a space for employees to connect, share experiences, and advocate for their needs.

Enhancing Employee Satisfaction and Retention

When employees feel understood, valued, and included, they are more likely to be satisfied with their jobs and remain with the organization. Empathetic and inclusive leadership creates a positive work environment where employees feel supported and engaged.

Increased Job Satisfaction: When employers actively listen to employees and value their contributions, employees are more likely to be satisfied with their work. This leads to higher levels of engagement and productivity.

Reduced Turnover: Inclusive workplaces have lower turnover rates, as employees are more likely to stay with organizations that respect and value them. This reduces recruitment and training costs and helps maintain organizational stability.

Driving Innovation and Performance

Diverse teams bring a wide range of perspectives and ideas, which can drive innovation and improve organizational performance. Inclusive leaders who foster a culture of collaboration and respect enable their teams to leverage this diversity effectively. Diverse teams bring a wide range of perspectives and ideas, which can drive innovation and improve organizational performance by:

Enhanced Problem-Solving: Diverse teams are better equipped to solve complex problems, as they can draw on a broader range of experiences and viewpoints. This leads to more creative and effective solutions.

Improved Decision-Making: Inclusive decision-making processes that involve diverse perspectives are likely to result in better outcomes. This is because they consider a wider range of factors and potential effects.

Greater Adaptability: Organizations that embrace diversity and inclusivity are more adaptable. They can better navigate changes and challenges by drawing on the strengths and insights of a diverse workforce.

Building a Strong Organizational Culture

Empathy and inclusivity are foundational elements of a strong organizational culture. When an organization genuinely embeds these values in its fabric, they influence behaviors, attitudes, and interactions at all levels. Leaders prioritizing empathy and inclusivity create workplaces where collaboration flourishes, reputations soar, and achieving long-term success is possible.

Cohesive and Collaborative Environment

A culture rooted in empathy and inclusivity fosters collaboration and teamwork. In this environment, employees of all backgrounds feel connected and motivated to work together towards shared goals. Valuing employees' voices and contributions creates a sense of purpose that transcends individual roles. Teams develop trust, share ideas, and support each other through challenges.

To build this environment, leaders need to go beyond the surface. Assuming that everything is running smoothly based on reports or metrics is not enough. Instead, they must get out from behind their desks and actively engage with their teams. Walk the floor. Sit in on team meetings. Observe the dynamics firsthand. Genuine conversations with employees across all levels reveal the heartbeat of an organization.

Take the time to talk to individuals two or three levels below you. Seek feedback from those who might not typically have a direct line to leadership. What's working? What isn't? For instance, a conversation with an intern at the end of their time with the organization can be a goldmine of insights. Interns often have fresh perspectives, unfiltered by years of organizational norms, and their feedback can shine a light on both strengths and areas for improvement.

These interactions aren't just about gathering information. They're about demonstrating that leadership genuinely cares. When all employees, regardless of their status or background, feel heard, they become more engaged, more motivated, and more willing to collaborate. This builds a sense of unity and shared purpose, essential ingredients for a cohesive and collaborative workplace.

Positive Employer Brand

Organizations that prioritize empathy and inclusivity are viewed positively by both current and potential employees. How a company respects, values, and supports individuals crucially influences its ability to attract top talent. Employees today are increasingly discerning. They want to work for organizations that reflect their values and where they feel they can thrive authentically.

How the outside world perceives an organization is just as important as have a strong organizational cultural inside of the company. When leaders actively engage with their teams, support diversity, and foster inclusivity, potential employees see that the company is a place where people, not the bottom line, come first. This reputation enhances the organization's ability to recruit and keep talent, positioning it as an employer of choice.

Long-Term Success

Empathy and inclusivity are not just about feel-good initiatives; they are strategic imperatives that drive long-term success. Organizations that embrace these values are better equipped to navigate the complexities of a global and dynamic business environment. Diverse and inclusive teams bring a wealth of perspectives, enabling companies to approach challenges with creativity and adaptability.

Building an empathetic and inclusive culture takes time and intentionality, but the rewards are profound. Such a culture fosters a resilient organization, motivates employees to perform better and empowers them to innovate. Leaders who regularly connect with their teams, act on feedback, and foster inclusion are laying the foundation for sustainable success ensuring that their organization thrives not just today, but well into the future.

The Future of Empathy and Inclusivity in Leadership

As the global business environment becomes increasingly diverse and interconnected, the importance of empathy and inclusivity in leadership continues to grow. The need for these qualities is further highlighted by emerging trends, such as remote work, digital transformation, and corporate social responsibility (CSR).

Remote work requires leaders to maintain open and empathetic communication in order to maintain connections and ensure that team members feel valued despite physical distance. Digital transformation brings opportunities to enhance collaboration but also demands careful navigation of ethical considerations like privacy and responsible technology use. CSR underscores the importance of ethical leadership, as stakeholders increasingly seek organizations committed to social and environmental responsibility.

By embracing empathy and inclusivity, leaders can build cultures of trust, collaboration, and innovation that drive long-term success in both remote and in-person environments. While the journey toward empathetic leadership is ongoing, the rewards in employee engagement, organizational performance, and meaningful impact are bountiful.

Unified Action Guide: Practical Steps for Empathy and Inclusivity

Empathy and inclusivity are foundational to effective leadership and shape how leaders connect with their teams and approach decisions. These values build trust, create fairness, and empower innovation. While the benefits are clear, putting them into practice requires intentional and consistent effort.

This Unified Action Guide provides practical steps to help leaders incorporate empathy and inclusivity into their daily leadership style. Each step is actionable, manageable, and designed to create a lasting impact. By applying these practices, leaders transform their teams into environments where every member feels valued, heard, and empowered.

Leadership is shaped by the small, daily actions that build a culture of care and collaboration. The steps that follow outline key focus areas, providing a road-map for fostering meaningful empathy and inclusivity.

---

1. **Practice Active Listening:** Empathy begins with truly hearing and understanding your team members. Active listening goes beyond simply hearing words because it requires you to engage with the speaker's emotions and intent.
    - **Be Present:** Eliminate distractions during conversations. Put down your phone, close your laptop, and focus fully on the person speaking.
    - **Ask Open-Ended Questions:** Invite deeper dialogue with questions like, "How do you feel about this approach?" or "What challenges are you facing right now?"
    - **Reflect and paraphrase:** Show understanding by restating key points. For example, "It sounds like you're feeling overwhelmed with competing deadlines. Is that right?"

   Active listening shows genuine care and creates an environment where team members feel valued.

---

2. **Empower Marginalized Voices:** Inclusivity isn't just about hiring diverse teams. As a leader, you need to ensure all of your team members feel valued by keeping them engaged and helping them thrive. Research published in Harvard Business Review found that employees who experience a strong sense of belonging at work show a 56% increase in job performance,

a 50% reduction in turnover risk, and a 75% decrease in sick days (Carr, E. et al., 2019). This underscores that investing in inclusivity and belonging isn't just about representation—it's about building stronger, more committed teams that perform better and stay longer.

To achieve this, leaders must actively empower marginalized voices in day-to-day interactions, meetings, and decision-making. This requires intentional leadership practices, such as:

- **Rotate Leadership Roles:** Assign quieter team members facilitation responsibilities in meetings to build their confidence and encourage active participation.
- **Proactively solicit input**—Directly invite feedback from those who may be less vocal in group settings to ensure that we hear and value a diversity of perspectives.
- **Establish Mentorship Programs**—Pair underrepresented team members with senior leaders who will advocate for their growth and support their professional development.
- **Build Inclusivity into Leadership Training**—We must have more than good intentions when it comes to empowering diverse voices; Integrate them into leadership development.
- **Offer Leadership Training Focused on Inclusive Communication**—Teach leaders how to listen actively, facilitate diverse discussions, and foster psychological safety.
- Hold bias awareness workshops to assist managers in recognizing and correcting unconscious biases within hiring, promotions, and team dynamics.
- **Foster Inclusive Growth Opportunities**—Ensure that all employees have equal access to career development programs, leadership tracks, and mentorship initiatives.

By implementing these strategies, inclusivity stops being just a discussion point and becomes an everyday practice that strengthens engagement, innovation, and long-term success.

---

3. **Celebrate Contributions and Successes:** Recognition plays a vital role in the realm of inclusive leadership. Team members are more engaged and motivated to contribute when leaders acknowledge their efforts. Here are two ways you can celebrate success:

    - **Acknowledge Unique Contributions**: Begin meetings with "shout outs", such as, "I appreciated Alex's creative problem-solving in yesterday's discussion."
    - **Celebrate Milestones**: Publicly recognize achievements of all sizes, whether it's a project delivered on time, a fresh perspective that sparked innovation, or a work anniversary for a team member.

    Regularly celebrating successes reinforces a culture where people feel seen and valued for their unique contributions.

---

4. **Foster Open Dialogue and Psychological Safety:** A truly inclusive environment encourages honest communication and respects diverse perspectives.

    - **Start with a Check-In**: Open team meetings with a roundtable question like, "What's one thing you're focusing on this week?" This sets the tone for openness and collaboration.
    - **Model Vulnerability**: Encourage others to share their challenges and uncertainties by modeling vulnerability yourself.
    - **Respect Differences**: Acknowledge when perspectives diverge and emphasize the value of diverse ideas in solving problems.

Psychological safety is imperative for people to feel safe expressing themselves without fear of judgment or retaliation. Harvard Business School professor Amy Edmondson's research on psychological safety found that teams with a strong sense of psychological safety outperform others because without fear or punishment or embarrassment, individuals feel comfortable speaking up.

When employees hesitate to share their perspectives, teams miss out on innovation and problem-solving opportunities. As leaders, we can cultivate psychological safety by actively listening, showing vulnerability, and creating an environment that welcomes diverse perspectives instead of dismissing them. One way to do this is by regularly asking open-ended questions, such as:

- "What's a perspective we haven't considered yet?"
- "What challenges are we overlooking?"

These changes create a workplace where employees feel valued which leads to greater engagement, retention, and team success.

---

5. **Challenge Bias and Build Awareness:** Inclusivity requires leaders to reflect on their own biases and actively work to counteract them.

    - **Implement Blind Hiring Practices**: Remove identifying details from resumes to focus on skills and experience.
    - **Seek Diverse Input**: Before deciding, consult stakeholders with diverse perspectives to ensure well-rounded solutions.
    - **Pause and Reflect**: Ask yourself, "Am I considering all perspectives, or just the ones that align with my own?"

Leaders must promote and practice fairness and provide opportunities for all voices to flourish by confronting biases.

---

6. **Make Empathy and Inclusivity Daily Habits:** Small, consistent actions compound over time to create lasting cultural change.
    - **Regular Check-Ins:** Ask team members how they're doing and what support they need. A simple "How can I help today?" can make a big difference.
    - **Walk the Floor:** Connect with employees in their workspaces, showing interest in their experiences.
    - **Solicit Feedback:** Regularly invite input on how inclusive your leadership feels and adjust accordingly.

    These daily practices not only build trust but also show your commitment to creating an inclusive environment.

Empathy and inclusivity are ongoing commitments that shape the heart of effective leadership. By focusing on these actionable steps, you'll foster stronger connections, inspire innovation, and build a culture where every individual feels valued and empowered to contribute. When practiced consistently, empathy and inclusivity transform teams into communities of growth, purpose, and success.

Final Thoughts on Empathy and Inclusivity

Empathy and inclusivity are not just ideals—they are deeply integrated into the foundation of meaningful and impactful leadership. Leaders who practice empathy create spaces where trust flourishes, connections deepen, and potential is unlocked. Those who prioritize inclusivity empower every individual to contribute their unique perspectives, building workplaces that thrive on diversity and innovation.

The impact of these values extends far beyond the team. When leaders model empathy and inclusivity, they create cultures where respect and collaboration become second nature. Employees carry these lessons into their interactions with clients, customers, and communities, amplifying the influence of inclusive leadership. This is how small, consistent actions ripple outward, shaping not just workplaces but the broader world.

Of course, leading with empathy and inclusivity is not without its challenges. Tight deadlines, complex decisions, and personal biases can test even the most well-intentioned leaders. In these moments that commitment matters most. Leadership that is rooted in empathy and inclusivity allows you to show up with authenticity, learn from missteps, and continuously grow thanks to input of a valued and diverse team.

Consider how you can bring these principles to life. Are you listening deeply to your team? Are you creating spaces for every voice to contribute? Are you celebrating differences that strengthen your team? These choices define a leader's legacy.

Leadership is a journey, and empathy and inclusivity are your compass. They guide you toward decisions that build trust, foster growth, and inspire change. By embracing these values, you're not just achieving results—you're creating a culture where people thrive, and innovation flourishes.

Empathetic and inclusive leadership is about putting people before profit. It's measured in the trust you build, the voices you amplify, and the culture you create. Lead with authenticity and let empathy and inclusivity become part of your legacy.

9

The Moral Compass

Leadership often demands that we navigate the intersection of authenticity and morality. This is a delicate balance between staying true to ourselves and meeting the ethical responsibilities of our roles. We celebrate authenticity as a powerful force because it fosters trust, drives genuine connections, and encourages a culture where people feel empowered to be themselves. But authenticity alone is not enough. Without morality as an anchor, authenticity can veer into territory that undermines trust, creates harm, or prioritizes self-interest over the greater good.

The idea of a moral compass serving as a guiding force to ensure that our actions are not just authentic but also ethical is essential. This moral compass directs us toward decisions that align with core values while respecting the perspectives and well-being of others. For leaders, this interplay is especially significant because their decisions have far-reaching consequences that shape organizational culture and influence the lives of those they lead.

Aligning authenticity with morality is rarely straightforward. Staying authentic when our values align with societal norms or when decisions don't involve tough trade-offs is easy. The real challenge comes when authenticity leads us to decisions that conflict with widely held beliefs or require navigating moral gray areas. Consider a leader who values transparency but must balance this with the need for confidentiality in sensitive situations. Their authenticity might urge them to disclose as much as possible, but their moral obligation to protect others may require restraint.

This chapter explores these challenges and opportunities through the lens of real-world examples, philosophical insights, and practical strategies. We'll examine how leaders can use authenticity to build trust and foster dialogue, while also ensuring their actions reflect a commitment to ethical principles. From navigating cultural differences in morality to understanding the consequences of acting authentically with flawed intentions, this chapter provides a road-map for meaningfully integrating authenticity and morality.

Ultimately, authenticity and morality are not opposing forces; they are complementary. Together, they form a framework for leadership that is both genuine and responsible. As we delve into the intricacies of this dynamic, consider how your own moral compass guides your authenticity. Are you leading with integrity, empathy, and accountability or do you need to put in some work in these areas?

Defining Authenticity and Morality

At its core, authenticity means being true to yourself. When you shed all masks and societal expectations, your lack of pretense shows who you truly are. Imagine someone who embraces their quirks unapologetically, whether it's their unconventional leadership style or their knack for telling dad jokes during tense meetings. Authenticity is about showing up as the real you, regardless of whether it fits neatly into the boxes others might prefer.

This concept resonates deeply in leadership because it cultivates trust. People gravitate toward leaders who are genuine and don't morph into what they think others want them to be. Authenticity says, "Here's who I am, and I'm okay with it." When others see that, they're more likely to feel okay being themselves, too. This creates an environment of openness where innovation and connection can thrive.

But authenticity, on its own, is not enough to effectively guide actions. Enter morality—the guiding principles that shape the intentions behind what we do. If authenticity is about *how* we interact, morality is the *why*. It's the compass that directs us by helping us decide what's right, fair, and just. While authenticity ensures we're true to ourselves, morality ensures we're accountable to others and to the world at large (Avolio & Gardner, 2005).

This distinction between authenticity and morality is critical. One can act authentically by aligning their actions with their internal beliefs while still causing harm. For example, someone who believes in ruthless competition may authentically pursue their goals with single-minded focus, but their actions might leave others hurt or disenfranchised. In such cases, the person's authenticity is intact, but their morality might be called into question. Being authentic isn't a free pass to be an "authentic asshole". Authenticity without morality is just an unchecked ego.

Consider this analogy: Authenticity is like a car's engine, driving actions forward with power and purpose. Morality is the GPS, providing direction to ensure the journey leads to a meaningful and ethical destination. Without the engine, you don't move. Without the GPS, you might move, but toward the wrong place.

In leadership, these two forces must work in tandem. A leader who is authentic but lacks moral grounding might earn trust initially, but risks misusing it. Conversely, a leader with strong moral convictions but no authenticity may struggle to inspire or connect with others. The magic happens when leaders integrate both, using authenticity to build genuine relationships and morality to make decisions that uphold shared values.

Maintaining balance in today's complex world is not always easy. It requires self-awareness, reflection, and willingness to adjust when needed. However, leaders who prioritize authenticity and morality reap abundant rewards when they create workplace cultures built on trust, respect, and shared purpose.

When you bring your true self to the table and align your actions with a moral framework, you create an environment where authenticity and morality thrive in harmony.

The Interplay of Authenticity and Morality

The relationship between authenticity and morality is both intricate and profound. We celebrate authenticity for its power to foster trust and connection, and its value can shift depending on the ethical lens through which it's viewed. Authenticity and morality operate on different planes: one governs how we act, while the other defines why we act. Together, they form a complex interplay that shapes the way others perceive our actions and the impact those actions have on the world.

Authenticity begins with the consistency of aligning one's actions with internal beliefs and values. At first glance, this might seem like an unequivocal virtue. After all, acting under your principles reflects honesty and transparency. But what happens when those principles are ethically questionable? For example, someone who firmly believes in prioritizing personal success above all else might act in a way that is wholly authentic but leaves others feeling undervalued or exploited. In such cases, authenticity ensures self-alignment but also exposes the potential disconnect between personal beliefs and societal norms.

Transparency adds another layer to this dynamic. Being open about one's intentions, whether altruistic or self-serving, can foster clarity and, sometimes, respect. However, this can backfire if one is too transparent. Imagine a leader who openly states that they are laying off employees to protect the company's bottom line. While we appreciate their honesty, the decision might still spark ethical concerns or backlash. Even when the rationale is clear, the action may still feel cold, impersonal, or misaligned with the company's stated values, especially if it appears to prioritize profits over people. This underscores an important truth: transparency makes actions more understandable, but it doesn't inherently make them morally right.

The tension becomes even greater when being true to one's principles leads to harmful outcomes. Acting authentically in alignment with values like *survival of the fittest* or *profit at any cost* might resonate deeply with someone's sense of self, but these principles can create conflict or damage relationships. While the individual may feel they are leading with integrity, others may view their actions as misguided or harmful. It's a sobering reminder that principles, however strongly held, are not exempt from moral and ethical scrutiny.

Society's perception of authenticity is an important aspect of this interplay. People are attracted to authenticity that aligns with positive intentions. On one hand, leaders who promote inclusivity, empathy, and fairness not only show alignment with our values, but also support societal ideals of what is good and just. On the other hand, self-serving or destructive motives may drive authenticity, and while its boldness might earn admiration, it often creates alienation and diminishes trust. The key difference is whether authenticity builds connections or causes division.

Ultimately, the interplay of authenticity and morality challenges us to think critically about the actions we take and the motivations behind them. Authenticity devoid of morality risks emptiness, whereas morality lacking authenticity struggles to motivate. Moral leadership requires an internal compass that prioritizes fairness, empathy, and responsibility, even when it's inconvenient or unpopular. It's not just about doing what feels right to you, but about doing what is right for others. When morality is detached from authenticity, actions can feel performative or hollow, driven more by optics than conviction. But when leaders align genuine intent with ethical standards, their decisions inspire trust and showcase integrity. Together, these forces guide leaders toward decisions that not only reflect their true selves but also contribute to a greater good. For leaders, navigating this balance is essential for creating a culture of trust and a meaningful impact.

Examples of Authenticity and Morality in Action

Real-world examples often provide the clearest lens through which to examine the interplay between authenticity and morality. These stories illuminate how authenticity can drive bold actions, but they also reveal the ethical complexities that arise when morality comes into question. Edward Snowden and Elizabeth Holmes are two particularly thought-provoking examples that illustrate this dynamic's profound impact.

Edward Snowden: Authenticity in Questioning Power

Edward Snowden's decision to leak classified information about the U.S. National Security Agency's (NSA) surveillance programs remains one of the most polarizing acts of the 21st century. At its heart, his story is one of authenticity colliding with established power structures.

Snowden deeply believed that the NSA's practices were unethical and violated the privacy rights of millions of individuals worldwide. His moral framework, rooted in transparency and accountability, left him unable to reconcile the agency's actions with his own values. Acting in alignment with those beliefs, and fully aware of the personal consequences of his decision, Snowden leaked classified documents to journalists (Greenwald et al., 2013). This act of authenticity where he put his principles above his own safety embodied a profound commitment to his moral compass.

Yet, people have fiercely debated the morality of Snowden's actions. To his supporters, he is a whistle-blower, a hero standing up for individual freedoms and democratic principles. To his detractors, he is a traitor who jeopardized national security and endangered lives. While we cannot deny the authenticity of his actions in that Snowden acted transparently and consistently with his deeply held convictions, in doing so, he risked our national security and violated a moral that most Americans hold in high regard. His example underscores the potential for authenticity to inspire significant change, even when the morality of the act is subject to debate.

Elizabeth Holmes: Ambition Unchecked

In stark contrast to Snowden's moral dilemma, Elizabeth Holmes provides an example of how authenticity, when paired with flawed morality, can lead to harm. As the founder of Theranos, Holmes captivated the world with her vision of revolutionizing healthcare through affordable, accessible diagnostic technology. Her ambition and drive were unmistakably authentic—she genuinely believed in the transformative potential of her vision and worked tirelessly to bring it to life.

However, the morality of her actions unraveled as her claims about Theranos's technology were not grounded in reality. Her claims misled investors, patients, and the public about the company's capabilities, endangering lives through inaccurate medical results (Carreyrou, 2018). Holmes built her pursuit of her vision, however intensely authentic, on deception.

Her story is a stark reminder that authenticity without moral grounding can lead to catastrophic outcomes. While her genuine belief in her mission might have driven her forward, the lack of ethical accountability undermined everything she sought to achieve. Holmes's downfall highlights the critical importance of aligning authenticity with a sound moral compass.

The Takeaway

These examples showcase two sides of the authenticity-morality equation. Edward Snowden's actions show how authenticity, even when controversial, can lead to meaningful societal conversations about ethics and accountability. Elizabeth Holmes, on the other hand, reveals how authenticity, when untethered from ethical principles, can cause harm and breaks trust.

For leaders, these stories serve as powerful reminders of the responsibility that comes with authenticity. Acting in alignment with one's beliefs is not enough; we must also scrutinize those beliefs through a moral lens. When authenticity and morality work together, the results can inspire trust, drive innovation, and create a lasting impact. When they diverge, the consequences can be just as powerful and destroy everything you've worked for.

The Complexity of Moral Diversity

Moral diversity is a defining characteristic of human interaction that reflects the wide range of values, beliefs, and ethical frameworks that shape our decisions. While authenticity asks us to remain true to our personal values, morality asks us to use societal norms to decide what is right and what is wrong within our culture and community while introducing a layer of complexity that challenges us to navigate differences with empathy and respect. The variety of moral compasses across cultures, philosophies, and individual experiences creates both opportunities for understanding and potential for conflicts.

Cultural and philosophical traditions have a big impact on ethical frameworks. Certain societies focus on the well-being of the community and make choices that benefit the larger group. In contrast, some societies prioritize individual autonomy, leading to a different view of what is considered right. Utilitarianism emphasizes the greatest good for the greatest number, while deontological ethics stresses strict adherence to rules. These distinctions show that morality is understood differently by different people, and there is no universal agreement on what is considered moral.

Personal experiences, education, and reasoning often lead individuals to different conclusions about what actions are justified or ethical. Imagine a scenario in which two leaders face the same dilemma of whether to lay off employees during an economic downturn. Though they both value their team members, one might see layoffs as a necessary step to preserve long-term stability, acting authentically according to his pragmatic principles. The other might prioritize maintaining employment at all costs, believing it to be a moral obligation to keep her team intact. Both are acting authentically, yet their moral judgments diverge significantly. This variability underscores the inherent subjectivity of moral interpretation.

One of the most significant challenges in navigating moral diversity is applying the same logic to others that we use for ourselves. Labeling actions as "wrong" when they conflict with our own values is easy, especially when those actions shape different cultural or religious contexts. However, such judgments often oversimplify the complexities at play. Consider a business practice viewed as standard in one country but deemed unethical in another. For example, giving small facilitation payments to expedite services, which is customary and legal in parts of Southeast Asia and the Middle East is considered bribery in the United States or most of Europe (except maybe in New York City or Chicago— just kidding…). Leaders in these situations must strive to understand the values driving the behavior, rather than defaulting to condemnation. Doing so requires not only openness but also a willingness to seek common ground.

Empathy plays a critical role in bridging these gaps. By stepping outside of our own perspectives and truly considering the experiences and motivations of others, we can navigate moral diversity with greater understanding and respect. This approach is important for leaders managing global teams or engaging in cross-cultural negotiations. Empathy allows them to foster collaboration, build trust, and create environments that value differing perspectives rather than dismiss them.

Ultimately, moral diversity is both a challenge and a strength. It asks us to hold firm to our authenticity while remaining open to the values and beliefs of others. Navigating this complexity requires humility and a commitment to understanding, but also offers an opportunity to learn, grow, and strengthen our connections with others. Authenticity paired with respect for moral diversity creates a foundation for meaningful dialogue and collaboration in an increasingly interconnected world.

Examples of Moral Complexity

Moral complexity occurs when conflicting values create tension that leads to tough decisions with no apparent right or wrong answers. These dilemmas show the complex connection between authenticity, morality, and the impact of our actions. Looking at real-life examples, like environmental ethics debates, social policies, and business practices, reveals the intricate challenges that leaders and individuals encounter when dealing with this complexity.

Environmental ethics often embody the struggle between economic growth and sustainability. For example, a company might consider expanding operations into a new market, promising increased profits and job creation. However, the expansion could also lead to significant environmental degradation, such as deforestation or pollution. A leader authentically focused on economic growth might justify the expansion as essential for stakeholders and regional development.

Conversely, a leader authentically committed to sustainability might prioritize environmental preservation, even at the expense of economic gains. Both positions reflect authentic values, yet the conflict between them illustrates how moral priorities can diverge in ways that are difficult to reconcile.

Social policies offer another lens through which to view moral complexity, particularly in the debate over welfare programs. One perspective sees welfare as a tool of social justice, ensuring that vulnerable populations receive the support they need to lead dignified lives. Authentic leaders who defend this view might advocate for expanded welfare initiatives, aligning with their belief in fairness and collective responsibility. Others might argue that welfare creates dependency while discouraging personal responsibility and long-term economic self-sufficiency. Leaders who authentically prioritize self-reliance might push for policies that reward work and reduce welfare dependency. Both positions reflect deeply held values, but the clash between them underscores the difficulty of creating policies that satisfy competing moral frameworks.

The tension between maximizing shareholder value and embracing social responsibility creates moral dilemmas within business practices. A CEO authentically dedicated to delivering financial returns might focus on cutting costs, streamlining operations, or prioritizing shareholder dividends, even if those actions negatively affect employees or communities. Meanwhile, a leader authentically committed to social responsibility might prioritize fair wages, environmentally friendly practices, or community engagement, even if it results in reduced short-term profits. Both approaches stem from genuine beliefs about what makes up effective leadership, yet they reveal the inherent trade-offs that leaders must navigate in the face of competing obligations.

These examples show that moral complexity often arises when authenticity collides with conflicting ethical priorities. Leaders who stay true to their values in these situations may still face criticism from those who hold different perspectives. The key to navigating such dilemmas lies in recognizing that moral complexity is not a weakness, but a natural part of decision-making in a diverse and interconnected world. By approaching these challenges with humility, empathy, and a willingness to engage in open dialogue, leaders can make thoughtful decisions that balance authenticity with the greater good.

The examples of moral complexity in environmental ethics, social policies, and business practices remind us that tough questions don't have simple answers. Authenticity is important, but we also need to understand that ethical tensions may arise and, as leaders, we will need to address them. Leaders must navigate these complexities with integrity and purpose.

The Complexity of Authentic Bad Intentions

We often celebrate authenticity as a virtue, but its impact significantly depends on the intentions motivating it. Troubling consequences arise when internal desires clash with societal standards or when people express authenticity without ethical grounding. The complexity of "authentic bad intentions" lies in the tension between acting true to oneself and the potential harm that such authenticity can cause.

One dimension of this complexity is the inner conflict that arises when personal desires run counter to societal norms or ethical expectations. Cognitive dissonance—the psychological discomfort caused by holding conflicting values or beliefs—often emerges in these situations. For instance, someone may authentically desire personal gain above all else yet feel guilt when those actions negatively impact others. This internal tension can create a struggle between being true to oneself and adhering to what society deems morally acceptable. The resolution of this conflict often defines how authenticity and morality interact in practice.

Another challenge lies in the ethical conundrum posed by authenticity itself. While authenticity encourages people to act in alignment with their beliefs, it does not automatically validate the morality of those beliefs. For example, a leader who authentically prioritizes profit over employee well-being may feel justified in their actions of hiring underqualified people at a lower wage, yet those decisions could lead to significant harm. Authenticity in this case ensures alignment with personal principles but does not shield the leader from ethical scrutiny. This illustrates a key limitation of authenticity: it is a vehicle for self-expression, but it cannot excuse harmful actions.

The distinction between authenticity and moral relativism adds further complexity. Authenticity asks us to stay true to our beliefs, but it does not imply that all beliefs are equally valid or beneficial. Moral relativism, the idea that no single moral framework is superior, can blur the lines between authenticity and ethical accountability. Uber's former CEO, Travis Kalanick, led with unfiltered intensity and a deep belief in disruption at any cost. His actions were fully aligned with his personal convictions. While his actions were undoubtedly authentic, they also fostered a toxic culture and eroded trust. (Lorenzo, R. et al., 2018) When authenticity becomes a shield for harm, it stops being a virtue and starts sounding like an excuse. Being true to yourself doesn't absolve you from the consequences of your actions—nor does it protect your beliefs from scrutiny.

This interplay reveals an important truth: pairing authenticity with a sound moral compass will have a positive impact. Acting authentically without regard for the ethical implications can lead to isolation, conflict, or harm. Conversely, balancing authenticity with ethical reflection allows individuals to navigate their inner desires while remaining accountable to the greater good.

Authentic bad intentions are complex. They show us that authenticity is powerful, but not always virtuous. While authenticity reflects who we are we need morality to guide us. This ensures that authenticity builds trust, connection, and positive results. Leaders who understand this balance can handle the ethical challenges of authenticity and make responsible decisions.

Authenticity and Moral Conflict

Authenticity often plays a pivotal role in navigating moral conflicts, acting as both a catalyst for transparency and a source of tension when values diverge. The open expression of one's beliefs can foster clarity and understanding, yet it also carries the risk of deepening divides. The challenge lies in balancing authenticity with an awareness of when and how to engage in conversations where moral perspectives differ.

Authenticity can serve as a powerful tool for transparent moral dialogue. Being honest about values and intentions lays the foundation for more meaningful discussions. In leadership, for example, a leader who openly shares their ethical reasoning behind a decision, even one that may be unpopular, demonstrates respect for their audience's intelligence and values. This kind of openness not only clarifies the decision-making process but also encourages others to express their views authentically, creating space for constructive dialogue.

However, the very act of expressing authentic beliefs can sometimes lead to conflict, especially when values diverge significantly. In polarizing discussions, such as debates over societal issues or organizational ethics, authenticity can expose the depth of moral divides. While openness is essential for addressing difficult topics, it also carries the risk of alienation. People may feel defensive or judged when confronted with beliefs that challenge their own, leading to tension rather than resolution. This is a critical juncture where leaders must navigate the fine line between authenticity and maintaining productive relationships.

The concept of ethical pluralism further underscores the importance of respecting diverse moral views. Ethical pluralism recognizes that people can hold legitimate, yet conflicting, moral perspectives shaped by their unique backgrounds and experiences. Rather than striving for universal agreement, this approach emphasizes coexistence and mutual respect. Authenticity within this framework means expressing one's beliefs clearly while remaining open to the perspectives of others. Leaders who embrace ethical pluralism create environments where diverse viewpoints, collaboration, and innovation thrive despite differences.

Ultimately, authenticity and moral conflict are deeply intertwined. While authentic expression is driven by honesty, we must also be sensitive to the complexities of moral diversity. By recognizing when to speak up and when to step back, and by fostering respect for differing values, leaders can navigate conflicts with grace and build stronger, more inclusive relationships. This balance allows authenticity to serve not as a source of division but as a bridge to greater understanding.

Practical Applications for Leaders

For leaders, the relationship between authenticity and morality isn't just theoretical. It shows up in how meetings are led, decisions are made, and company culture is shaped.

Use the following strategies to apply authentic, ethical leadership in your day-to-day:

---

1. **Align decisions with personal and organizational values:** Authentic leaders consistently check their moral compass and ensure their choices reflect not just what feels right to them, but also what aligns with the organization's mission. For example, a leader who values fairness and equality may routinely review compensation models to ensure all roles are in-line with industry standards, not just high-profile roles.

---

2. **Pause and weigh competing values before acting:** When facing complex decisions, resist the urge to default to your first instinct. Authenticity encourages personal truth, but morality requires reflection on broader impact. For instance, a leader may personally value speed and efficiency but should pause to consider inclusivity and thoroughness before pushing for rapid change without soliciting additional input.

---

3. **Foster a culture of moral dialogue:** Encourage open discussions about ethical dilemmas, personal values during team retrospectives or leadership meetings. Create psychological safety by acknowledging that differing views don't need to lead to division—they can drive better decisions. A leader grounded in humility and curiosity sets the tone for respectful debate.

---

4. **Be selective and intentional in what you share:** Authenticity doesn't mean narrating every twist and turn of the decision-making process. While sharing that you are exploring shifts or acknowledging you are working on a problem that everyone is expecting you to solve is okay and even encouraged, sharing too early before plans are fully formed can create confusion or give the impression that leadership is indecisive. Instead, wait until strategies are finalized and then communicate them. This approach ensures clarity, reinforces confidence in leadership, and prevents unnecessary speculation. Now that these decisions are solidified, you should share them transparently, explaining the rationale and anticipated impact. This balance fosters trust and demonstrates thoughtful leadership.

---

5. **Reinforce consistency through behavior, not just words:** Authenticity isn't about making grand declarations at the quarterly town hall meetings; it's about how you show up, especially when no one's watching. Leaders who prioritize morality are role models for ethical behavior in everything from how they handle feedback to how they treat junior staff.

When leaders put these principles into practice, they're leading with intention and not just trying to be authentic. Staying grounded in your values, weighing tough trade-offs, encouraging open dialogue, and knowing when to speak up and when to hold back are all skills that build something far bigger than just personal credibility: they are creating trust. When you lead this way, people notice. They trust more, contribute more, and stick around longer. Authenticity turns into impact.

Final Thoughts

As we close this chapter, it's worth reflecting on the dual power of authenticity and morality in leadership. Together, they enable trust, accountability, and meaningful impact. However, neither operates effectively in isolation. Authenticity without morality risks being self-centered, while morality without authenticity can feel rigid or impersonal. Leadership demands a careful balancing act that requires thoughtfulness and intention in order to integrate both.

One of the important points of this exploration is the importance of a strong moral compass. A moral compass is not just a tool for making decisions; it is a lens through which we view the world and our responsibilities within it. It helps leaders stay grounded, ensuring that their actions align with their values and contribute to the greater good. But a moral compass is not static—it requires regular recalibration. Life is dynamic, and leaders must adapt to new challenges, diverse perspectives, and developing circumstances without losing sight of their principles.

Leaders should understand the importance of dialogue in moral situations. Leading is not a solo effort, and moral decision-making can benefit from others' input. People will feel safe to express their views on such sensitive topics when their leader has created a safe environment for collaboration while reinforcing the ethical foundations of the organization. These leaders embrace the opinions of others and have set the tone for a culture where integrity and authenticity thrive.

Navigating moral complexity is also a critical skill. The examples in this chapter highlight how moral dilemmas are rarely black and white. Whether balancing economic growth with sustainability, shareholder value with social responsibility, or transparency with confidentiality, leaders must weigh competing priorities with care. These situations test not only a leader's decision-making ability but also their capacity for empathy and humility. Recognizing that there may not always be a clear "right" answer is part of the journey.

Finally, remember that leading with authenticity and morality is not about perfection. Leaders will inevitably face missteps or moments of doubt. What matters is their willingness to learn, adapt, and recommit to their values. Even though you won't have all of the answers, being honest about your intentions, transparent about your decisions, and accountable for your actions helps build your authenticity.

As you continue your leadership journey, think about how you can strengthen the connection between your authenticity and your moral compass. What legacy do you want to leave? How can your leadership inspire trust, foster inclusivity, and drive positive change? By staying true to yourself and aligning your actions with ethical principles, you can create a lasting impact that extends far beyond your immediate sphere of influence. In the end, the most effective leaders are those who lead not just with authenticity but with integrity, empathy, and a deep commitment to the greater good.

10

Overcoming Challenges

"It's easy to be captain of the ship when the sea is calm" is a phrase we've all heard and commonly holds true. However, times of crisis truly test a leader's abilities. When challenges arise, such as sudden disruptions, long-term changes, or unexpected setbacks, a leader's ability to navigate uncertainty becomes crucial and is the compass that guides their team. These moments are not just about managing logistics or solving immediate problems. They are about setting a tone, building trust, and inspiring resilience.

Effective leadership during a crisis requires more than just a simple strategy; it demands a leader who is emotionally intelligent, aware of both their own emotions and those of their team. The ability to recognize, understand, and manage emotions plays a pivotal role in guiding teams through uncertainty.

In times of crisis, people look to their leaders not just for answers, but for stability, empathy, and purpose. They want to believe their leader understands the gravity of the situation and is dedicated to guiding them through it, for both the organization and team. Leaders who can tune into the emotions of their team, acknowledge concerns, and respond with empathy create a foundation of trust and psychological safety (A. Edmondson, 1999). Teams confidently face even the most difficult situations when they are supported by a leader who understands and values their emotions.

This chapter explores what it means to lead with authenticity during challenging times. At its heart is the understanding that resilience is a collective endeavor built on trust, communication, and a shared sense of purpose. Leaders play a pivotal role in creating an environment where teams feel supported, empowered, and connected, even when the path ahead is uncertain.

Steadfastness in the Storm

When everything feels like it's falling apart, when challenges are piling up and uncertainty looms, it's easy for teams to feel adrift. That's when an authentic leader truly shines. Consider a lighthouse weathering a tempest. Its light is steadfast, dependable, and a constant guide to everything around it. Authentic leaders don't just weather the storm; they become the lighthouse, a source of calm and direction for everyone around them.

The secret? Stay grounded in your values. In chaotic moments, chasing quick fixes or reacting impulsively is tempting. But authentic leaders know their values are like an anchor that keeps them focused and steady no matter how rough the waters get. When your team sees you holding firm you reassure them that while everything else might feel unpredictable, there's a clear and consistent set of values guiding the ship.

Let's talk about communication. Being transparent when the news isn't good is difficult, right? Even so, keep in mind that people can handle, and prefer, the truth. What they can't handle being left in the dark. Authentic leaders know that honesty, even in uncomfortable situations, is non-negotiable. Sharing what's going on and, just as importantly, what's being done about it builds trust. It's like saying, "I see the challenges, too, and we're in this together." That openness turns anxiety into action and speculation into problem-solving.

Empathy also plays a big role here. Crises don't just impact schedules and bottom lines—they affect people. Stress, fear, frustration are all part of the mix. An outstanding leader doesn't brush those emotions aside. Instead, they acknowledge them. Maybe it's as simple as saying, "I know this is tough, and I'm feeling it too," or taking time to really listen when someone shares their concerns. The smallest connections can be incredibly significant. They remind your team that they're not just cogs in a machine and that they're valued, and their feelings matter.

Let's not forget the importance of consistency. During a storm, the last thing a team needs is a leader who wavers or sends mixed signals. Consistency builds confidence and shows your team that you're not just making decisions on a whim but that you are staying true to the values and vision you've always stood for. That doesn't mean pretending everything's fine—it's about being steady and intentional, even when the path forward isn't perfectly clear.

Speaking of the path forward, clarity is everything. When overwhelmed, people easily lose sight of the bigger picture. That's where you come in. Your job as a leader is to cut through the noise and provide direction. What's the goal? What's the plan? Even if the plan might evolve, having something tangible to rally around gives your team purpose and focus. It's like saying, "Here is where we're going, and here is how we're going to get there together."

Now, it's important to highlight that being steadfast doesn't mean being rigid. Staying true to your values is one thing but being flexible in how you approach challenges is equally important. Effective leaders combine consistent practices with the ability to adapt. They're not afraid to pivot if the situation calls for it, and they're open to ideas from their team. This mix of stability and flexibility encourages innovation and shows that you trust your people to help navigate the storm.

The real magic of leadership that is steadfast, is that it leaves a lasting impact. How you show up during the tough times sets the tone for how your team tackles challenges in the future. When they see you leading with honesty, empathy, and resilience, they are inspired to adopt those qualities, too. It's like planting seeds of trust and courage that grow well beyond the immediate crisis.

Being steadfast in the storm isn't about pretending you have all the answers. It's about showing up authentically, staying true to your values, and guiding your team with courage and clarity. That's what makes the difference—not just surviving the storm but coming out the other side stronger, more united, and ready for whatever comes next.

Communicating with Clarity and Compassion

In times of crisis or change, communication becomes more than just the transmission of information—it's a lifeline. Authentic leaders know their words and actions have a tremendous impact, shaping how people perceive and manage situations. Clear and compassionate communication is the cornerstone of this process, ensuring transparency, honesty, and emotional sensitivity at every turn.

Effective communication depends on honesty and transparency. While you might want to soften bad news or avoid hard truths altogether, authentic leaders resist this urge. Truth, even when unpleasant, builds trust and authentic leaders understand this. Whether the message involves setbacks, restructuring, or uncertainty, delivering clear and accurate information ensures that team members feel respected and informed. This honesty reinforces the leader's credibility and builds a culture where openness becomes the norm.

Honesty alone isn't enough. During turbulent times, people need more than just facts—they need empathy and sensitivity. Authentic leaders recognize crises impact individuals differently, triggering stress, fear, or frustration. By acknowledging these emotions and showing genuine care, leaders create a supportive environment. Simple acts, like taking the time to ask, "How are you holding up?" or validating concerns with statements such as, "I know this situation is difficult for everyone," go a long way in building trust and connection.

However, as an authentic leader, you can't just ask a connecting question and walk away. We all know a person who asks a question like this with the sole intent of getting your answer out of the way so they can begin telling you what they have to say. Take the time to truly listen, show empathy, and follow up on supportive actions you commit to. These small moments of compassion remind the team that their well-being, not just their productivity, is a priority.

Equally important is the consistency of communication. Uncertainty festers in silence, and when people feel left in the dark, their fears can grow unchecked. That's why regular updates are critical. Authentic leaders establish reliable channels for sharing information, whether through team meetings, emails, or one-on-one check-ins. These updates need to convey progress, next steps, and a commitment to keeping the team informed. Consistent communication creates a sense of continuity, reducing uncertainty and reinforcing the idea that the leader is engaged in addressing the challenges at hand.

Authentic leaders also tailor their communication styles to the moment. In high-stakes scenarios, brevity and clarity are often the best approach. In a crisis moment, you may need to stick with a concise update to convey what you know, here's what you're doing, what comes next. However, when emotions are running high, you'll need to take a more conversational tone to address underlying fears or frustrations. Adjusting the approach shows adaptability and a nuanced understanding of what the situation demands.

Listening is another essential component of clear and compassionate communication. Though leadership is in charge of delivering messages, it is also responsible for creating space for team members to voice their concerns and ideas. Authentic leaders actively listen and that they value input and are open to feedback. This two-way dialogue fosters collaboration and ensures that the communication process feels inclusive rather than one-sided.

A practical example of compassionate communication in action could be a leader addressing a significant change, such as a departmental restructuring. Instead of simply announcing the decision, they might begin by explaining the context: "We've been facing financial pressures that require us to adapt." They would then share the decision itself, emphasizing its rationale: "To remain sustainable, we're merging teams and reallocating resources." Finally, they would acknowledge the emotional impact: "I know this news may feel overwhelming. I want to assure you we're here to support you through these changes."

Ultimately, the goal of clear and compassionate communication is to bridge the gap between uncertainty and understanding. When team members feel informed, heard, and supported, they are better equipped to navigate the challenges ahead. Authentic leaders who prioritize transparency, empathy, and consistency not only guide their teams through difficult times but also strengthen the bonds of trust and resilience that will endure long after the crisis has passed.

Empathy and Emotional Intelligence in Crisis Leadership

In times of uncertainty, it's not just the tactical decisions that matter but also how leaders connect with their teams on an emotional level. Leaders who lead with authenticity recognize the importance of emotional intelligence (EQ) as a key tool for navigating crises. Recognizing, understanding, and managing your own emotions and those of others is a skill that helps leaders respond to their team's emotional needs while maintaining clarity and focus on the larger mission.

Research has shown that emotional intelligence directly correlates with effective leadership, especially when managing a crisis. A meta-analysis published in the Leadership & Organization Development Journal (2019) revealed an interesting statistic: leaders with higher EQ scores led teams that were 29% more likely to display resilience and 36% more likely to perform well under pressure during challenging situations. The study emphasizes that when leaders are aware of their own emotional responses and can empathize with their team's concerns; they create an environment where people feel supported and equipped to tackle challenges.

This is especially important in crisis situations, where stress and uncertainty are heightened. It's easy for leaders to become consumed by the immediate need to act, but EQ allows them to pause, reflect, and make decisions that consider both the emotional and practical needs of the team. Authentic leaders are not just about managing logistics. They are leading with compassion and understanding, which fosters a sense of psychological safety and trust.

Leaders who exhibit high emotional intelligence address the emotional undercurrents of a crisis. Whether it's reassuring a worried team member, helping the team manage frustration, or simply listening to concerns, these leaders create an atmosphere where people feel heard and understood. This can significantly reduce anxiety, creating the mental space needed for individuals to focus on solutions rather than fears.

As an authentic leader, your ability to tune into both your own emotions and those of your team isn't just a leadership asset; it's an emotional safeguard for the people you're guiding. Your ability to remain calm, empathetic, and emotionally present will help your team navigate the storm with resilience and confidence.

Being Present and Accessible

In times of crisis, a leader's presence can feel like a lifeline to their team. Whether you're showing up physically or virtually in a remote work environment, being truly present and accessible in a way that reassures, supports, and inspires confidence brings a calm in times of crisis. When uncertainty looms, authentic leaders recognize that their visibility and approachability are crucial to maintaining trust and morale.

Visibility is the first step to being present. Don't just show your face during team meetings. Make sure your team sees you engaged in managing the situation. Whether it's through regular virtual check-ins, impromptu conversations, or walking the floor if possible, your visibility sends a simple message that you are here, you are involved, and you care about what happens next. Leaders who make themselves seen regularly and stay actively engaged remind their teams that they aren't navigating the storm alone.

Visibility isn't just about frequency—it's about quality. Showing up should feel purposeful, not performative. If you're in a meeting, are you genuinely engaged, or are you distracted by other responsibilities? Are you listening intently to team concerns, or are you rushing through your updates? Authentic leaders understand that their presence is most impactful when it feels intentional. Active listening and addressing concerns during a 15-minute check-in is more effective at boosting morale than an hour-long meeting with divided attention.

Accessibility goes hand in hand with visibility. Visibility means very little if you are not also approachable. Accessibility means creating opportunities for team members to share their thoughts, ask questions, or simply seek reassurance. This might involve maintaining an open-door policy, offering scheduled one-on-one meetings, or making yourself available for informal chats. The key is to meet your team where they are, both physically and emotionally.

Another practical approach to this might look like a leader setting aside "office hours" for team members to drop in virtually or in person with questions. It could also involve regularly scheduled updates where the leader not only shares news but actively invites feedback. Simply walking around the office or hosting informal virtual hangouts in a remote environment, and engaging in casual conversations that keep the lines of communication open is another effective way to be accessible to team members.

One important aspect of accessibility is balancing availability with boundaries. While being there for your team is vital, overextending yourself to the point of burnout helps no one. Authentic leaders communicate their limits clearly and model healthy work habits which shows their teams that it's okay to set boundaries while still being supportive and engaged.

Being accessible also means embracing humility. Leaders who admit when they don't have all the answers or acknowledge when they're feeling the strain themselves can foster deeper connections with their teams. This kind of openness breaks down hierarchies and reminds everyone that leadership is as much about being human as it is about decision-making.

During crises, we must remember that visibility and accessibility work together to create a sense of solidarity. A leader who is present and approachable shows their commitment to the team which reinforces a culture of trust and unity. When people see their leader actively involved, they are reassured because someone is steering the ship. When they know they can share their concerns openly, they feel valued and heard.

Ultimately, being present and accessible isn't about grand gestures but about showing up consistently and authentically in order to create spaces where your team feels supported, you address concerns promptly, and the human connection is never lost, even amid chaos. Leaders who prioritize these principles lay the groundwork for trust, collaboration, and resilience that will sustain their teams long after the immediate crisis has passed.

Simply Be a Good Human

In times of crisis, leadership isn't about delivering polished speeches or executing perfect plans—it's about being real. Your team needs to know, without a doubt, that you're not just another voice echoing the company line. They need to believe you are speaking from the heart, with their best interests in mind. Being human—genuinely, unapologetically human—is one of the most powerful tools a leader can wield during challenging times.

To be human is to embrace vulnerability. No one expects you to have all the answers, and pretending otherwise can erode trust. Admitting uncertainty by saying, "I don't know, but here's how we're working to find out," shows your team that you're honest and approachable. This openness fosters a sense of shared experience. It tells your team that you are all in the situation together and that you value their trust enough to be candid

Being human also means balancing transparency with empathy. While it's important to share the truth, it's equally important to deliver it in a way that acknowledges the emotional weight of the moment. For example, instead of saying, "This project failed, and we need to move on," you might say, "I know this outcome is disappointing, and it's okay to feel frustrated. Here's what we can learn from this, and how we can move forward together." Framing challenges in a way that validates emotions helps your team process setbacks without feeling dismissed.

Authentic leaders recognize that their humanity is more relatable than their title. Little things like checking in on a stressed team member, admitting your own struggles, or even sharing a personal story about overcoming difficulty creates genuine connections. These moments remind your team that you're not just their boss; your someone who genuinely understands their challenges.

Another essential aspect of being a good human is resisting the temptation to shield yourself with corporate jargon or impersonal messaging. Don't fall into the trap of saying what you think your team wants to hear because those words often come across as insincere. Instead, speak plainly and from the heart. If budget cuts are necessary, don't sugarcoat the decision. Explain the why. Describe your feelings about it. Let your team see the person behind the decision.

Finally, being a good person means showing your team that you care about them as people, not just staff. Just ask, "How are you holding up?" and really listen to the answer. Make space for your team to voice concerns without fear of judgment. Treat each person with respect and show that their happiness is as important as the company's profits. The old adage of 'treat others how you want to be treated' goes a long way in terms of being a decent person.

When leaders embrace their humanity, they inspire trust, loyalty, and resilience. Your team needs someone who navigates challenges with integrity, communicates with empathy, and builds trust through authenticity. By simply being human, you remind your team members that even in the hardest times, they're not alone.

Empowering Teams to Adapt

Change and uncertainty often bring an initial wave of hesitation or resistance, but they also create opportunities for growth and innovation. A leader's ability to empower their team to adapt during these times is critical. Authentic leaders recognize that adaptation isn't about forcing people to conform to a new reality but about enabling them to find their footing, embrace challenges, and develop creative solutions which gives your teams autonomy and flexibility. By doing this, leaders help their teams not just survive but thrive in the face of change.

To empower teams, start by encouraging innovation. Authentic leaders understand new challenges need fresh perspectives. This involves creating a safe environment for team members to share ideas, even unconventional ones. Psychological safety is crucial. When the fear of judgement is eliminated from a situation, people think more creatively. A leader can say, "There's no wrong answer. What's your boldest idea?" This simple invitation promotes creative problem-solving and boosts team members' confidence to contribute meaningfully.

Once the ideas start flowing, it's important to encourage flexibility. Adapting to change means recognizing that there's rarely a single right way forward. Teams need the freedom to adjust their strategies and experiment with different approaches. For example, if a traditional workflow no longer meets the demands of a new situation, an authentic leader might encourage the team to reimagine their processes. This might involve piloting a new tool or restructuring roles temporarily to meet immediate needs. Leaders play a crucial role in supporting this flexibility by ensuring their teams have the resources, time, and autonomy to explore new possibilities.

Flexibility also requires leaders to model adaptability themselves. If team members see their leader pivoting gracefully in response to setbacks or challenges, they're more likely to follow suit. Adapting in a crisis is as much about mindset as it is strategy. By showing that flexibility is a strength, not a compromise, leaders set the tone for an adaptive, resilient team culture.

Trust is what allows teams to adapt effectively. Trusting your team to take ownership of their tasks and decisions is empowering and lets your team know that you believe in their ability to handle the situation. To cultivate this trust, leaders must delegate responsibility thoughtfully, allowing team members to take charge of specific aspects of a project or a challenge. Micromanagement stifles creativity and erodes confidence, so it's essential to balance oversight and autonomy. Checking in periodically is important, but those check-ins should focus on support rather than control.

Another powerful way to build trust is by providing clear direction without dictating every detail. For example, a leader might outline a challenge and say, "Here's the outcome we need to achieve. I trust you to determine the best way to get us there. Let me know how I can help along the way." This approach gives the team both a logical goal and the freedom to innovate, empowering them to take initiative and adapt their methods as needed while leadership steps back in order to avoid micromanaging.

Authentic leaders also understand the importance of celebrating small wins along the way. Adaptation is often a process of trial and error and recognizing progress, however incremental, keeps morale high and momentum going. A simple acknowledgment like, "That solved a tough problem," reinforces the value of innovation and effort while encouraging the team to keep pushing forward.

Lastly, leaders must be prepared to guide their teams in reflecting on the adaptation process. After navigating a challenge, take a moment to reflect back on what worked, what didn't, and what was learned. These reflections not only help refine future approaches but also highlight the team's growth and resilience. Team members seeing how their efforts contributed to overcoming obstacles reinforces their sense of capability and prepares them to tackle future changes with confidence.

In the end, empowering teams to creates prime conditions for growth. By encouraging innovation, fostering flexibility, and building trust, leaders inspire their teams approach challenges with creativity and resilience. Adaptation becomes not just a reaction to change, but a skill that strengthens the team for whatever comes next.

Enhance Team Cohesion and Morale

In challenging times, a cohesive and motivated team can make all the difference. Resilient leadership plays a pivotal role in fostering a sense of unity and shared purpose. When leaders show adaptability and resilience, they model behaviors that inspire their teams to collaborate more effectively, creating a stronger, more connected dynamic.

Building unity starts with a culture of mutual support and collaboration. Teams thrive when every member feels valued and knows their contributions matter. Leaders can nurture this by creating opportunities for open communication, encouraging team members to share ideas, asking questions, and providing feedback without fear of judgment. For example, starting meetings with a quick roundtable check-in allows everyone to feel heard and promotes transparency. Recognizing individual and collective contributions, whether it's a quick thank-you during a meeting or a public acknowledgment of a job well done, reinforces the idea that everyone's efforts are vital to the team's success.

A shared purpose is also key to cohesion. Leaders can strengthen unity by reminding their teams of the bigger picture. Whether it's completing a critical project, navigating a crisis, or achieving long-term goals, connecting daily tasks to a greater mission helps teams stay focused and aligned. Sometimes, reminding people that what they are working on in the here and now isn't just solving a problem for the time being, but that they are laying the groundwork for future success.

Boosting morale goes hand in hand with building unity. A leader's attitude sets the tone for the entire team. When leaders approach challenges with positivity and a focus on solutions, their teams are inspired to adopt the same mindset. This doesn't mean ignoring difficulties. Rather, it's about framing setbacks as opportunities to learn and grow. When something doesn't go as planned, the authentic leader reflects on what can be taken away from the experience in order to improve the next time

Celebrating successes, no matter how small, can also have a big impact on morale. Whether it's hitting a milestone, overcoming a tough hurdle, or simply acknowledging the team's hard work, these celebrations remind people of their progress and keep spirits high. Leaders should make a point to recognize wins both publicly and privately, tailoring their approach to what resonates best with their team.

By prioritizing unity and morale, leaders create an environment where teams can weather challenges together, emerging stronger, more resilient, and ready to tackle what lies ahead.

Set a Precedent for Future Challenges

How leaders respond to today's crises doesn't just solve immediate problems. Your response sets the tone for how their teams will face challenges in the future. Resilient leadership establishes a culture that doesn't view obstacles as roadblocks, but as opportunities to learn, grow, and innovate. This mindset drives an organization's long-term success.

The first step in building this mindset is promoting a positive culture around challenges. Leaders have the power to shape how their teams perceive adversity. By framing challenges as opportunities, they encourage a mindset of resilience and adaptability. For example, a leader might say, "This situation is tough, but it's also a chance for us to rethink how we work and come out stronger." This perspective helps reduce fear and fosters curiosity and creativity instead.

Recognition of and rewarding resilience is another key to establishing this culture. When team members step up to tackle difficult situations, leaders should acknowledge their efforts. Publicly celebrating those who show adaptability reinforces the value of these behaviors, which encourages others to follow suit. This might look like highlighting a team member's innovative solution during a meeting or simply sending a personal note of appreciation. Over time, this practice signals that resilience and problem-solving aren't just appreciated—they're expected and integral to the organization's DNA.

Equally important is encouraging continuous improvement. Challenges often reveal areas where processes, skills, or strategies need refinement. Authentic leaders use these moments as learning opportunities, guiding their teams to reflect on what worked, what didn't, and how to improve. Ask: "How might we use this experience and its lessons the next time?"

Building a feedback loop into their team's operations allows for continuous improvement. Regularly inviting input from team members and being open to change ensures that the organization stays agile and ready for what's next. For instance, after overcoming a major obstacle, a leader might hold a debrief session to collect insights and actions for future scenarios.

By promoting a positive culture and prioritizing growth, leaders set a precedent that transforms how their teams approach challenges. Instead of fearing the unknown, teams learn to see it as an opportunity to adapt and excel, ensuring the organization's resilience far into the future.

Final Thoughts: A Leadership Legacy of Resilience

Leading through crises isn't just about solving immediate problems—it's about shaping a legacy of resilience, trust, and authenticity. Each decision, conversation, and action shapes how we will approach challenges now and in the future. Authentic leaders understand their role goes beyond managing outcomes and is about connecting with their teams on a deeply human level and guiding them with integrity and compassion.

Leaders need to be present and accessible to establish a connection. When they engage with their teams, they show commitment and solidarity. Showing up, focusing, and addressing concerns are not minor acts, but profound gestures that build trust and foster unity.

Effective communication strengthens those connections. Speaking with clarity and compassion provides the transparency teams need to understand and adapt to challenges. Leaders who are honest, empathetic, and consistent in their messaging reduce uncertainty and inspire collective problem-solving.

At the heart of resilient leadership, however, is humanity. Approach every interaction honestly, vulnerably, and with genuine care. Show your team that you aren't just a boss—you're a leader who understands their struggles and values their contributions. When teams believe in their leader's authenticity, they are more willing to step up, adapt, and push through adversity.

Emotional intelligence (EQ) is a core component of this leadership style. Leaders who show empathy and emotional awareness create an environment where their teams feel supported and understood, even during crises. Again, emotionally intelligent leaders are 29% more likely to foster resilience and 36% more likely to guide their teams to higher performance under pressure. This ability to connect emotionally helps build the trust and flexibility needed to navigate the challenges of today—and those of the future.

Trust enables teams to adapt and grow. By encouraging innovation, fostering flexibility, and trusting their capabilities, leaders unlock the creative potential within their teams. This empowerment isn't just a response to immediate challenges but an investment in the future, preparing the organization to thrive in a world of constant change.

Finally, today's crisis leadership sets a precedent for approaching future challenges. Framing obstacles as opportunities for growth creates a culture of resilience and continuous improvement, ensuring the organization remains agile and forward-thinking.

Leadership during tough times isn't about perfection—it's about authenticity, showing up with integrity, empowering others, and leading with humanity. The legacy of resilient leadership is reflected in teams that trust, adapt, and thrive together, not just through the storm but long after it has passed.

11

"The 48 Laws of Authenticity"

What if the most powerful leaders are the ones who don't seek power at all? For decades, leaders have been told that control, secrecy, and ruthless ambition are the keys to success. The book *The 48 Laws of Power* by Robert Greene describes power as a competition where manipulation is effective and trust is a weakness (Greene, 2000). Despite Greene's attempts to reduce our human history to a series of power-hungry moguls, the most influential, respected, and enduring leaders didn't achieve success by outmaneuvering and deceiving others. They succeed by building something that lasts.

Power tactics are insanely seductive. Who wouldn't want to guarantee their own dominance by following laws like "Crush Your Enemy Totally" or "Conceal Your Intentions"? But here's the problem: deception-based power is fleeting and crumbles when trust vanishes.

Authenticity, unlike traditional views of power, thrives not in complexity, but in simplicity, transparency, and enduring trust. Greene's *48 Laws* guide us through intricate tactics of manipulation and strategic control, yet authenticity doesn't play by these rules. It doesn't require dozens of complicated laws. Instead, authenticity flourishes with clarity and intentionality.

The difference between manipulation and authentic leadership is simple: one aims to impress, the other aims to endure. A leader who rules through secrecy and control may look powerful, but their influence is like a sandcastle before high tide—temporary and fragile. As we've explored, authentic leadership builds rock-solid trust and genuine purpose, designed to withstand any storm.

The laws of power should prioritize connection over deception and cultivate real influence instead of focusing on control. Leaders who want to create lasting impact focus on inspiring their team members through consistency, trust, and maintaining their values because an authentic leader knows that power built through manipulation fades quickly, but power rooted in authenticity stands the test of time.

Why Power-Seeking Leadership Fails

Greene's *The 48 Laws of Power* thrives on strategic maneuvering, often at the expense of trust and relationships. These tactics, like the ones listed below, may deliver quick wins, but they create long-term instability.

Mistrust Accumulates: Manipulation breeds paranoia. Employees, partners, and peers may comply in the short term, but they won't invest their loyalty in someone they can't trust.

Short-Term Gains, Long-Term Losses: Winning by deception mirrors playing poker with marked cards—eventually, people catch on, and the house always wins.

The Isolation Problem: The higher you climb through fear and manipulation, the lonelier life gets. Authentic leaders build networks of genuine support that sustain them through challenges.

The Manipulative Magician

Let's return to my favorite super-villain in the book. Nobody would be surprised if Elizabeth Holmes had *The 48 Laws of Power* on her nightstand and studied it like a playbook for her rise in Silicon Valley. Her approach to leadership, storytelling, and deception aligned so perfectly with Greene's principles that it almost seems intentional. But as her story proves, following these laws to the letter doesn't guarantee lasting success. On the contrary, it often speeds up failure (Carreyrou, 2018).

Holmes built Theranos on a foundation of secrecy, illusion, and manipulation and executed several of Greene's laws with textbook precision. She mastered Law 6: Court Attention at All Costs, crafting a persona that made her appear larger than life. Holmes didn't just want to be another Silicon Valley CEO—she wanted to be the visionary of a generation. She went so far as to style herself after Steve Jobs and controlled every aspect of her public image, down to her deepened voice and signature black turtleneck.

Her rise was also driven by Law 3: Conceal Your Intentions. Holmes was notorious for keeping Theranos' technology hidden from scrutiny. She kept the inner workings of the company's blood-testing machines, the Eddison, hidden from employees, investors, and partners like Walgreens. She claimed that secrecy was necessary to protect proprietary technology, but in reality, it concealed the company's fatal flaw: the Edison didn't work.

When skepticism arose, Holmes turned to Law 15: Crush Your Enemy Totally. Holmes fired employees who questioned the technology behind the Edison. The company threatened whistle-blowers with legal action. She created a culture of fear, silencing dissenters before they could expose the truth. This iron-fisted control initially worked and allowed Theranos to continue raising millions in funding and securing high-profile board members like Henry Kissinger and George Shultz.

But manipulation has an expiration date. Holmes also embraced Law 27: Play on People's Need to Believe and exploited the hopes of patients, investors, and the media. She promised a revolution in healthcare and used emotionally charged language to convince people that Theranos was changing the world. Knowing that optimism often overrides skepticism, she preyed on the desire to believe in healthcare breakthroughs.

For a while, these tactics worked. Forbes and Time Magazine celebrated her as a pioneer. She secured partnerships with major pharmaceutical companies and attracted billions in investments. Unfortunately for Holmes, who followed Law 17: Keep Others in Suspended Terror, one can only sustain unpredictability and fear for so long before the illusion collapses.

Her empire unraveled when journalists and whistle-blowers exposed the truth. The Wall Street Journal revealed that Theranos' devices never worked as promised, and instead of acknowledging the company's failures, Holmes doubled down on deception. Even though she utilized Law 29: Plan All the Way to the End, her plan failed to account for the exposure of her lies.

Holmes used Greene's laws masterfully to gain power, but she never considered that power built on deception is temporary. She created an empire where fear replaced trust, secrecy replaced transparency, and illusion replaced authenticity. In the end, those choices sealed her fate.

Holmes' downfall serves as a cautionary tale, demonstrating that while manipulation may provide short-term success, it cannot sustain true leadership. Authentic leaders don't rely on fear or deception to gain influence. Instead, they earn it through trust, integrity, and delivering on their promises.

Her story is a stark contrast to those who embrace authenticity. While her empire collapsed under the weight of its own lies, leaders who build real trust create legacies that endure. Holmes' failure isn't just a scandal—it's proof that manipulation is a losing strategy in the long run.

Holmes followed *The 48 Laws of Power* to the letter. But the one universal leadership law she chose to ignore—the law of trust—is the one that mattered most.

"The 48 Laws of Authenticity": A Rebuttal to Manipulation

I don't have 48 laws in this book—just my top five. Why? Because quite frankly, leadership shouldn't be that complex. *The 48 Laws of Power* is a playbook for strategic manipulation, but I'd argue that true leadership doesn't require deception, secrecy, or crushing enemies.

So, consider these five laws as my best rebuttal. If *The 48 Laws of Power* is about mastering the art of control, "The 48 Laws of Authenticity" is about mastering the art of influence—the kind that doesn't require smoke and mirrors.

Authenticity Law 1: Lead with Transparency (vs. Law 3: Conceal Your Intentions)

Authentic leadership starts with the foundational principle of openness. Leaders who embrace transparency foster trust, ensure their intentions are clear, their actions visible, and their decision-making process is understandable to everyone involved. Rather than hiding behind secrets, they stand in the light and are willing to acknowledge both their strengths and their weaknesses.

A powerful example of this in action is Yvon Chouinard, the founder of Patagonia. Chouinard built Patagonia into a billion-dollar company by embedding transparency into every facet of the business, showing that profitability and sustainability can go hand-in-hand (King, 2024). Unlike many corporations that discreetly manage environmental effects to avoid scrutiny, Patagonia takes a radically honest approach and openly shares its challenges and progress toward sustainability. In 2011, the company even ran an ad during Black Friday that read, "Don't Buy This Jacket" in an effort to encourage consumers to buy less because every product made takes resources from the planet (Chouinard, 2006). Instead of damaging its brand, the ad underscored its commitment to sustainability and solidified Patagonia's reputation as a company driven by values rather than profits alone.

Chouinard's transparency extends beyond consumer-facing messages. Internally, he fostered a culture that encouraged employees to hold leadership accountable. The company openly discusses its sourcing practices and environmental footprint, which builds trust with customers and those within the organization. This kind of openness strengthens relationships, cultivates genuine loyalty, and creates an environment where employees feel empowered to contribute to the company's mission in meaningful ways. In contrast to Greene's Law 3, which promotes secrecy and concealment of intentions, authentic leaders like Chouinard build relationships that are rooted in openness, creating a resilient foundation for both business success and lasting trust.

Authenticity Law 2: Build Allies, Not Enemies (vs. Law 15: Crush Your Enemy Totally)

In Greene's world of strategic dominance, you must frame competition as an all-out war, where the aim is to crush rivals and eliminate any potential threats. However, authentic leadership rejects this zero-sum mentality, understanding that building sustainable success through collaboration, cooperation, and mutually beneficial relationships is the true mission. Instead of seeing competitors as enemies to defeat, authentic leaders recognize that partnerships, knowledge-sharing, and a spirit of "coopetition"—competing while cooperating—build thriving industries.

The tech sector, specifically the relationship between Apple and Samsung, provides a prime example of this. Though these companies are fierce competitors in the smartphone market, they also rely on each other for critical components. Samsung, a primary supplier of OLED screens and processors for Apple's devices, showcases how two businesses in direct competition can still cooperate in a way that fuels growth and innovation. Far from seeking to undermine each other, both companies benefit from this strategic collaboration, demonstrating that even in fiercely competitive markets, cooperation can lead to shared success.

Similarly, the automotive industry provides several examples of how coopetition has become a driver of long-term progress. Companies like Ford, General Motors, and Stellantis have come together to advance electric vehicle technology, co-developing solutions to reduce costs, share resources, and speed up the adoption of sustainable technologies. Initiatives like the Suppliers Partnership for the Environment (SP) demonstrate that addressing challenges like carbon reduction and supply chain sustainability is far more effective when competitors put aside their differences and collaborate for the greater good.

In this way, authentic leaders take a broader view of competition and see it not as a battle for dominance but as an opportunity for collaboration that enhances both their own success and that of the entire industry. The leaders who understand the power of building allies, rather than creating enemies, are the ones who establish long-term success that is not easily diminished by the rise or fall of individual competitors.

Authenticity Law 3: Inspire Through Purpose (vs. Law 27: Play on People's Need to Believe)

While Greene advocates manipulating people's desires and emotions for personal gain, authentic leadership relies on creating real, purpose-driven movements. Authentic leaders do not use empty promises or deceptive narratives to rally followers. They inspire through a clear and interesting vision that aligns with shared values. This is the leadership that generates genuine loyalty because it draws people not to a leader's image, but to the purpose that the leader represents.

A prime example of purpose-driven leadership is Alan Mulally's tenure as CEO of Ford. When Mulally took charge during one of the company's most challenging periods when Ford was facing declining sales, low morale, and an unclear future, he did not resort to gimmicks or emotional manipulation (Leggett, T., 2014). Instead, Mulally embraced radical transparency and instilled a sense of shared responsibility within the organization through his vision of One Ford. His leadership focused on the idea that Ford's success would not come from deception or onetime wins, but from building a culture of teamwork and collaboration, driven by a sense of common purpose.

Under Mulally's leadership, employees rallied around the belief that Ford could make it through the crisis by working together and innovating as a unified force. This clear, honest vision helped restore public trust, revitalized the company, and ultimately enabled Ford to avoid bankruptcy without relying on government bailouts. Mulally's ability to inspire through purpose, instead of manipulating beliefs, underscores the power of authentic leadership. Leaders who create alignment around shared values and goals do not need to prey on people's desire to believe; they inspire through substance and clarity.

Authenticity Law 4: Act with Adaptability, Not Just Boldness (vs. Law 28: Enter Action with Boldness)

Greene's call for bold, decisive action often promotes a mindset where leaders act with unwavering confidence, regardless of the situation. However, true leadership involves more than just boldness. It requires the wisdom to assess and adapt to changing circumstances. Boldness without adaptability can lead to rash decisions and unchecked consequences. Authentic leaders know that success isn't about charging ahead at all costs but about making informed decisions and being flexible enough to change direction when necessary.

A powerful example of this adaptability is New Zealand Prime Minister Jacinda Ardern's leadership throughout the COVID pandemic ("Coronavirus," 2020). While many world leaders hesitated to implement drastic measures, Ardern acted swiftly, imposing strict lockdowns to prevent the virus's spread. What set her apart, however, was her willingness to adapt to her approach based on new data and shifting circumstances. As the pandemic developed, Ardern showed an ability to adjust her policies without clinging to the initial decisions she had made. This adaptability, combined with transparency and inclusiveness, helped maintain public trust, a vital element of leadership during a crisis.

Similarly, Ardern's handling of the 2019 Christchurch, NZ mosque attacks showed her responsiveness to the needs of affected communities (Mercer, P., 2019). Rather than relying on political rhetoric or slow-moving bureaucratic processes, Ardern took immediate action to reform New Zealand's gun laws after listening to the survivors and the communities affected by the tragedy. Her ability to adapt, while maintaining her core values, exemplifies authentic leadership and underscores that boldness without flexibility can be reckless, but adaptability ensures resilience.

Authenticity Law 5: Strengthen the Team for Long-Term Success (vs. Law 42: Strike the Shepherd, Scatter the Sheep)

While Greene suggests eliminating key figures to destabilize opposition and consolidate control, authentic leadership takes a different approach. Rather than trying to undermine others, authentic leaders focus on empowering and strengthening their teams. They understand that the true strength of a leader lies in his ability to build resilient, collaborative teams, where each member feels valued and invested in the organization's mission.

Gregg Popovich, the legendary coach of the San Antonio Spurs, is a prime example of this leadership style. Instead of relying on superstar athletes or creating a culture of fear, Popovich built a dynasty by prioritizing team cohesion, player development, and mutual trust (Taylor, 2014). His leadership philosophy emphasized selfless basketball and a commitment to collective success. Popovich empowered his players, ensuring that each individual contributed to the team's success. Under his guidance, the Spurs won five championships without the need to rely on dominant superstars, proving that a team built on trust, respect, and collaboration is more sustainable than one dependent on control.

Similarly, Alan Mulally's approach to Ford focused on strengthening the company's internal culture rather than attacking competitors. His One

Ford vision broke down internal silos and encouraged employees across divisions to work together toward a common goal. This culture of collaboration, rather than division, played a crucial role in Ford's successful turnaround and long-term sustainability.

Instead of focusing on weakening rivals, authentic leaders strengthen their own teams by ensuring that everyone is invested in the mission. When a leader builds a powerful, empowered team, success focuses on creating a culture where collaboration drives long-term success, making competition and defeating others irrelevant.

Legacy Over Quick Wins

Power-seekers often focus on achieving dominance in the here and now, pursuing short-term victories that grant immediate recognition. But such power, rooted in deception, fear, or manipulation, is fragile. It's a fleeting form of success, dependent on maintaining control through tactics that ultimately erode trust and stifle growth. The moment these leaders falter, their influence crumbles—leaving behind only the ruins of their broken empire.

Authentic leadership is about creating a legacy rooted in values that will stand the test of time and transcends the leader's tenure. The most enduring leaders do not seek to accumulate power for power's sake. They focus on creating systems, teams, and cultures that continue to thrive long after they are gone. Trust, integrity, and empowering others, not manipulation, form the foundation of their enduring influence.

History is full of examples of leaders who prioritized short-term victories over long-term impact, only to see their influence fade as quickly as it appeared. Dictators, corporate tyrants, and egotistical executives may command obedience, which works for a while, but once their grip weakens, so does their power. Their legacies are marked by fear, control, and distrust. These qualities may bring fleeting success but will never withstand the test of time.

Nelson Mandela's legacy is one of reconciliation, collaboration, and empowerment. After 27 years of imprisonment, Mandela emerged not as a vengeful leader, but as one committed to healing a divided nation (Lopez, J., 2013). He understood that lasting leadership is not about punishment or dominance but about building bridges, fostering unity, and ensuring that the values you stand for live on through others. Mandela's true legacy lies not in his personal power, but in the systems and relationships he built that continue to shape South Africa today.

Mandela's leadership wasn't about achieving quick wins. His leadership created a foundation that withstands the trials of time, even as South Africa faces new leadership challenges today. His leadership empowered others to take action and created a country that could heal and grow. Unlike the Mandela Effect, which distorts his history, the reality of his leadership remains impossible to erase. His true legacy is clear in the people he served and the nation he helped to rebuild.

This principle applies just as much in business and leadership today. The most successful and respected leaders are not those who achieve quick, flashy wins or maintain control through fear and manipulation. They are the ones who build something greater than themselves, whether that's a resilient company culture, a movement that transcends the individual, or a team that continues to succeed long after the leader's involvement.

The best leaders know that trust is an asset, not a vulnerability. They invest in their teams, build lasting relationships, and ensure that their leadership is not about hoarding power, but about empowering others to thrive. By focusing on creating sustainable success, they forge a legacy that endures long beyond their time at the helm.

The choice is simple: do you want to build something that can be washed away with the tide, or a legacy that stands the test of time? Authentic leadership builds a foundation that won't crumble, that is enduring and lasting.

Final Thoughts: A Nod to Greene

While Robert Greene's *The 48 Laws of Power* has undeniably influenced the way we think about leadership and influence, his perspective on power is one of manipulation, secrecy, and control. Greene's ideas focus on the competitive aspects of leadership, showing how to win and maintain power in difficult circumstances. His insights have shaped the conversations around strategy and influence in business and society. His laws provide a road-map for leaders who want power at any cost.

However, there is another way. *The 48 Laws of Authenticity* present a radically different view that emphasizes trust, transparency, and long-term impact over short-term manipulation. Authentic leadership is about building something that lasts, not just winning in the moment. It's about inspiring others through purpose, adapting in the face of uncertainty, and empowering teams to succeed without relying on fear or deception.

The choice is simple: follow the path of control, secrecy, and manipulation, or choose authenticity and a path that fosters genuine trust, sustainable success, and builds a legacy. Authentic leaders do not hoard power; they share it, knowing that true influence comes not from dominance but from empowering others to lead alongside them.

Greene's laws may still resonate with some, but authenticity offers a model for leadership that creates a lasting impact. The leaders who act with integrity, invest in their people, and prioritize trust will leave an enduring legacy—not those who manipulate and deceive for temporary gain.

Authenticity isn't just an alternative to Greene's approach—it's the ultimate power move.

12

The Choice to Lead Authentically

We've explored the foundations of authentic leadership—self-awareness, integrity, trust, vulnerability, and resilience. You've read about what it means to lead with conviction, navigate challenges with transparency, and build meaningful connections with your team.

Now, will you actually lead this way when it counts?

Authenticity is easy when no one is watching and there's no risk, no consequence, no pressure to conform. But what about when the direction from the bosses above doesn't align with your values? When everyone around you is taking the easy way out? When doing the right thing might cost you your credibility, opportunity, or financial security? That's where the ultimate test of leadership happens. That's where you must make the choice to lead authentically.

Arlan Hamilton: A Lesson in Betting on Yourself

Arlan Hamilton didn't come from wealth, privilege, or the world of venture capital (Hamilton, A., 2020). She had no elite credentials, no industry connections, and no financial backing. In fact, when she started building *Backstage Capital*, she was homeless, sleeping in airports and borrowing money just to get by. But she had something even more powerful than resources: conviction. She saw a glaring inequity in venture capital where women, people of color, and LGBTQ+ founders were being shut out of funding not because of their ideas, but because they didn't fit Silicon Valley's mold. Rather than waiting for the system to change, she set out to change it herself.

Raising money without connections or wealth is nearly impossible. Arlan knew this. Instead of backing down, she bet on herself. She cold-emailed hundreds of investors, making the case that diverse founders weren't just deserving of funding—they were a smarter investment. Most ignored her. Some laughed. A few told her outright that she would fail.

She didn't stop. She documented every rejection, every small win, and every hard-earned lesson. Then, after months of relentless outreach, she secured her first $25,000 check that changed everything. That first investment became the catalyst for something bigger. Over time, she built relationships, leveraged credibility, and raised millions to launch *Backstage Capital*, a fund dedicated to investing in the very founders the industry overlooked.

Today, *Backstage Capital* has invested in over 200 companies, proving that betting on underrepresented founders isn't charity—it's good business ("Backstage Capital - For Investors," 2025). Arlan has become an author, a sought-after speaker, and one of the most influential voices in venture capital. While her story is about personal success, it highlights how reshaping an industry and proving that authenticity and conviction aren't just ideals—they're strategies for impact.

Authenticity as a Leadership Choice

Many leaders claim authenticity, but do they practice it when it's uncomfortable? The defining moments of leadership often come when there is a choice between what's easy and what's right. Staying true to one's values is not always the most profitable, efficient, or popular path in the short term.

Consider Arlan's journey. Traditional venture capitalists focus on founders who fit a specific mold—elite schools, established networks, and generational wealth. Hamilton had the choice to follow the same path and get funded faster, but she rejected that. Instead, she focused on her mission of funding founders who lacked opportunities elsewhere. Doing so wasn't the convenient choice, but it was the authentic one. And in the long run, it made all the difference.

Authenticity is not a passive trait—it's a deliberate decision made repeatedly in the face of pressure. Every leader will face these decision points. Do you compromise your values for an easier path? Or do you lean into authenticity, knowing the path might take longer or be more difficult?

Arlan's Inherent Leadership Principles

Arlan Hamilton's journey offers an interesting blueprint for what it means to lead authentically, even when the path is uncertain and the odds are against you. Her story is a testament to the power of standing firm in your values, and it perfectly reflects the authentic leadership principles we've explored throughout this book.

Defining Authentic Leadership (Chapter 1): Arlan didn't fit the mold of a typical venture capitalist. She had no financial backing, no elite connections, and no blueprint to follow. But she had a deep understanding of who she was and what she stood for. She didn't reshape herself to fit the expectations of Silicon Valley; instead, she leaned into her uniqueness and built something new. Her story is an example of what we discussed in Chapter 1—how self-awareness, transparency, integrity, and consistency form the foundation of authentic leadership.

Leading with Integrity (Chapter 3): We test integrity in moments when doing the right thing is hard. Arlan faced countless opportunities to abandon her mission in favor of faster funding or industry approval. Instead of focusing on the same founders as traditional VCs, she stayed true to her belief that underrepresented entrepreneurs have been unfairly shut out of funding opportunities. Her decision to stand firm reflects the core message of Chapter 3: authentic leaders don't just talk about their values—they act on them, even when it costs them in the short term.

Cultivating Trust and Transparency (Chapter 4): Arlan's radical transparency about the challenges of fundraising, the realities of being an outsider in venture capital, and the struggles of building a firm from scratch made her leadership style unique. She didn't hide her setbacks; she shared them. This openness not only built trust with the founders she backed but also with a broader audience who saw her as a leader willing to challenge the status quo. As we explored in Chapter 4, authenticity and transparency go hand in hand. Leaders who are honest about their journey earn deeper trust and loyalty from those they lead.

Overcoming Challenges (Chapter 10): If Arlan's journey proves anything, it's that rejection is not the end of the road—it's part of the process. Before she secured funding for Backstage Capital, she was turned down by nearly every major investor she pitched to. She faced closed doors, skepticism, and resistance. Many would have given up. Instead, she adjusted her approach without compromising her mission. This resilience is a cornerstone of authentic leadership in Chapter 10. Leaders who stay true to their purpose despite setbacks ultimately build something stronger and more meaningful.

Leading a Legacy of Authenticity (Chapter 11): Arlan's impact extends far beyond her own company. She didn't just create a venture capital firm. She changed the conversation about who gets funded and why. She built a model that others are now following, proving that diverse investment isn't just the right thing to do; it's a smart business strategy. As we explored in Chapter 11, true leadership isn't just about individual success—it's about leaving a lasting impact. Arlan's work continues to inspire a new generation of investors and entrepreneurs, prompting them to question and rethink traditional methods of opportunity allocation.

The Lasting Impact of Authentic Leadership

Authentic leadership is not just about personal integrity—it has a profound effect on organizations and the people within them. Leaders who embrace authenticity shape company culture, foster trust, and set new standards for their industry. Their influence extends beyond their immediate teams and ripples through the entire organization, creating long-lasting benefits that outlive their tenure.

Why does this matter?

Leadership decisions don't happen in a vacuum. The way a leader engages, communicates, and operates directly affects how employees feel about their work, their trust in the organization, and their motivation to contribute meaningfully.

Authentic leaders build empowered, motivated, and resilient teams. Employees feel valued and heard, which fosters higher engagement and productivity.

Integrity-driven leadership creates a ripple effect. Leaders who act with honesty and consistency inspire their teams to do the same, reinforcing a strong ethical culture throughout the organization.

Organizations led with authenticity thrive on trust. Transparency in leadership encourages open dialogue, minimizes internal politics, and nurtures a work environment where employees feel safe to take risks and innovate.

How Organizations Benefit

The impact of authentic leadership extends beyond individual influence and transforms companies into high-performing, values-driven organizations.

Businesses that prioritize authentic leadership see measurable advantages, including:

Increased employee engagement and retention. Workers are more likely to stay with organizations where leadership is transparent and value-driven. Employees who trust their leaders feel a greater sense of purpose and commitment to their work.

A culture of transparency and accountability. Organizations that operate with openness attract top talent who appreciate clear expectations, honest feedback, and a culture that values integrity.

A lasting leadership legacy. When you embed authenticity into the company culture, it doesn't disappear when one leader exits. Future leaders inherit and uphold the same values, ensuring long-term sustainability and impact.

Authentic leadership is more than a personal leadership style—it is a business strategy that creates lasting success at every level of an organization. By prioritizing integrity, trust, and transparency, leaders build companies that don't just perform well, but also stand the test of time.

Are You Leading Authentically?

Leadership isn't just about making decisions—it's about making the right decisions, even when it's difficult. This self-assessment helps you reflect on how authentically you lead.

How to Use This Assessment

Grab a piece of paper or open a notes app on your phone. Instead of marking directly in this book, record your answers elsewhere as you reflect. For each question, rate yourself on a scale of 1 to 5 (1 = Rarely, 5 = Always). Be honest—this is for you, and only you.

Self-Assessment: How Authentically Do You Lead?

Your Leadership Foundations

1. Do I make decisions based on my core values rather than on external pressure?
2. Do I encourage transparency and trust in my team, even when difficult?
3. Do I allow my true personality to come through in leadership moments?
4. Do I admit mistakes and show vulnerability when needed?
5. Do I prioritize long-term impact over short-term wins?

Your Influence on Others

1. Do my employees/team members feel comfortable giving me honest feedback?
2. Do I model the behaviors I expect from my team?
3. Do I listen more than I speak in team discussions?
4. Do I create an environment where people feel safe to take risks?
5. Do I make decisions with fairness and consistency?

Your Resilience & Growth

1. When facing external pressure, do I stay true to my leadership values?
2. Do I actively seek feedback to improve my leadership style?
3. Do I surround myself with people who challenge me to be better?
4. Do I take time for self-reflection and personal growth?
5. Do I remain authentic even in high-pressure situations?

Scoring and Interpretation

Calculate your total score for each section separately and then add them up to determine your overall score.

Leadership Foundations (Questions 1-5) Total:

Influence on Others (Questions 6-10) Total:

Resilience & Growth (Questions 11-15) Total:

Which section has your lowest score? That's where you have the most opportunity for growth. Focus your efforts on strengthening this area first.

Your Overall Authentic Leadership Score

Now, add the scores from all three sections to get a total score out of 75.

Score Range - Your Authentic Leadership Level

60-75 points: *Authenticity in Action*: You consistently lead with authenticity. Keep challenging yourself to refine your leadership and look for opportunities to mentor other leaders by sharing your experiences.

45-59 points: *Strong Intentions, Inconsistent Execution*: You value authenticity but struggle under pressure. Identify two areas where you can reinforce your values daily.

30-44 points: *Awareness Without Action*: You recognize authenticity's importance but hesitate to act. Start small—focus on a single improvement for 30 days.

Below 30 points: *Opportunity for Transformation*: Authenticity hasn't been your focus—yet. Start with daily check-ins and small but meaningful actions.

Let's break down each section individually. Find your weakest area based on your lowest score in either Leadership Foundations, Influence on Others, or Resilience & Growth. I'll summarize each category, and it's your responsibility to create a plan to improve your leadership skills in the areas that need the most focus. This book has covered all the information for each category, so now it's your turn to act.

Leadership Foundations: Developing strong leadership foundations starts with defining your core values and ensuring they guide every decision you make. Reflect on moments when you felt conflicted—were your choices aligned with your values? If not, what external pressures influenced you? Establish a habit of checking in with yourself before making key decisions to ensure they align with your authentic leadership style.

Influence on Others: Authentic leaders cultivate environments of trust, psychological safety, and meaningful connection. Start by assessing how openly your team communicates with you. Do they feel comfortable sharing concerns or providing feedback? Foster stronger trust through active listening, being transparent about decisions, and modeling vulnerability. The more trust you build, the stronger your leadership influence becomes.

Resilience & Growth: Leading authentically under pressure is one of the greatest challenges a leader can face. Identify specific situations where you compromise your authenticity, whether because of stress, external expectations, or fear of failure. Work on building resilience by setting clear personal boundaries, practicing emotional regulation techniques, and reminding yourself that authenticity strengthens rather than weakens your leadership in difficult moments.

Authenticity is about committing yourself to progress. Every choice you make as an authentic leader builds trust, strengthens your influence, and shapes the surrounding culture. Leadership is a journey, and authenticity is a daily practice. Consistently aligning your actions with your values, through small decisions, defines you as a leader. Growth comes from awareness, action, and accountability. Take ownership of your development, embrace challenges as opportunities, and lead in a way that inspires others to do the same. The path to authentic leadership is yours to walk—one intentional step at a time.

Next Steps: Strengthening Your Authentic Leadership

Authenticity is a continuous process of alignment between your values, actions, and leadership approach.

Here are practical ways to build and sustain authentic leadership:

Daily self-check-ins: Start each day by asking yourself, "Am I leading authentically today?" This simple reflection helps reinforce the habit of conscious, values-driven leadership.

Find accountability partners: Identify mentors, peers, or team members who will challenge and support you in staying true to your leadership values. Authenticity thrives when you have people who encourage you to uphold your principles, even in challenging situations.

Commit to continuous learning: Authentic leaders don't stagnate. Be open to feedback, engage in personal development, and be willing to adjust your approach when new insights emerge. Reading, mentorship, and coaching can all help refine your leadership style.

Resist external pressure: The easiest path is rarely the most authentic. Leadership often comes with pressure to conform, take shortcuts, or make decisions that are expedient rather than ethical. Develop strategies to maintain your integrity when facing external demands—whether it's setting boundaries, taking time to reflect, or seeking counsel from trusted advisors.

Lead by example: The best way to inspire authenticity in others is to model it yourself. When you consistently show authenticity through your words, actions, and leadership style, you give others permission to do the same.

Authentic leadership is a journey, not a destination. Every decision, conversation, and challenge presents an opportunity to align your actions with your values. Leadership is not about perfection, but about consistent effort and growth. The more you commit to leading with authenticity, the stronger and more lasting your impact will be.

The Final Call to Action: What Kind of Leader Will You Be?

You've taken this journey through the principles of authentic leadership. You've reflected on the importance of trust, transparency, and leading by example. You've examined how leaders like Arlan Hamilton made the hard choice to stay true to their values even when it was inconvenient. You've assessed your own leadership and identified areas for growth. What kind of leader will you be?

Authenticity isn't just a concept you've read about—it's your commitment to making it a daily practice. It's tested in moments when the simple path is tempting, when external pressures push you toward compromise, and when leadership requires courage rather than convenience. The most important step you can take now is to commit to action. Reflecting on authenticity is valuable, but what defines you is how you bring it to life in your leadership.

Your Leadership Commitments

Take a moment to answer these questions for yourself. Be specific. Write your answers down:

What three things will you change in your leadership starting tomorrow?

How will you hold yourself accountable to these changes?

Who will you invite into your leadership journey to ensure you stay on track?

One of the most powerful ways to hold yourself accountable in any personal transformation, whether it's learning a new skill or becoming a more authentic leader, is to share your journey with others. Studies have shown that individuals who publicly document their progress are more likely to stay committed because they create a sense of social accountability. The same principle applies to leadership growth. Openly communicating your intention to lead more authentically invites colleagues, mentors, and your team to help you stay on track.

This doesn't mean broadcasting every thought or struggle on social media, though that can work for some. Instead, be intentional in sharing your aspirations and commitments in spaces where accountability and support thrive. Maybe it's as simple as telling your team, "I'm working on being more transparent in my leadership, and I'd love your feedback if you ever feel I'm falling short." Or perhaps it's reflecting publicly in a professional network, posting about moments when authenticity challenged you and what you learned.

Authenticity isn't a switch you flip—it's a practice. That practice becomes real when witnessed. Witnessing your efforts will not only hold you accountable but will also inspire others to join you in leading with greater honesty and integrity. By sharing your journey, you don't just transform yourself, you create a ripple effect that redefines leadership culture around you.

Change doesn't happen all at once. Every decision you make either reinforces or weakens your commitment to authenticity. The leaders who leave a lasting impact are the ones who consistently align their values with their actions, even when it's difficult.

A Leadership Legacy That Matters

As you move forward, remember that leadership is more than your title, position, or authority. It's the influence you have on those around you. Your leadership leaves a mark on your team, your organization, and your industry. Make sure it's one worth remembering.

Authentic leadership isn't about getting things right every time. It's about showing up, making the hard but right decisions, and committing to being the leader people can trust. The world doesn't need more leaders who prioritize convenience over conviction. It needs leaders who will stand firm in what they believe, even when the path forward is uncertain.

You have the tools, the awareness, and the choice. The only question that remains is: Will you lead authentically?

Bibliography

Avolio, B. J., & Gardner, W. L. (2005). Authentic leadership development: Getting to the root of positive forms of leadership. *The Leadership Quarterly, 16*(3), 315–338. https://doi.org/10.1016/j.leaqua.2005.03.001

Backstage Capital—For Investors. (2025). *Backstage Capital.* https://backstagecapital.com/for-investors/

Brown, B. (Director). (2010, June). *The Power of Vulnerability* [Video]. https://www.ted.com/talks/brene_brown_the_power_of_vulnerability

Brown, B. (2018). *Dare to lead: Brave work, tough conversations, whole hearts.* Random House.

Carr, E., Reece, A., Rosen Kellerman, G., & Robichaux, A. (2019, December 16). *The Value of Belonging at Work.* Harvard Business Review. https://hbr.org/2019/12/the-value-of-belonging-at-work

Carreyrou, J. (2018). *Bad blood: Secrets and lies in a Silicon Valley Startup* (First Vintage Books Edition). Vintage Books, a division of Penguin Random House LLC.

Chamorro-Premuzic, T. & Buchband, R. (2020, December 23). *If You're Tracking Employee Behavior, Be Transparent About It.* Harvard Business Review. https://hbr.org/2020/12/if-youre-tracking-employee-behavior-be-transparent-about-it

Chouinard, Y. (2006). *Let my people go surfing: The education of a reluctant businessman.* Penguin Books.

Coronavirus: How New Zealand relied on science and empathy. (2020, April 20). *BBC News*. https://www.bbc.com/news/world-asia-52344299

Dartey-Baah, K., Issahaku, L., & Akwetey-Siaw, B. (2024). Authentic leadership and employee engagement: The mediating role of employee work environment. *Industrial and Commercial Training, 57*(1), 118–134. https://doi.org/10.1108/ICT-06-2024-0045

Edelman Trust Barometer. (2023). Edelman. Retrieved May 28, 2025, from https://www.edelman.com/trust/2023/trust-barometer

Edmondson, A. (1999). Psychological Safety and Learning Behavior in Work Teams. *Administrative Science Quarterly, 44*(2), 350–383. https://doi.org/10.2307/2666999

Edmondson, A. C., & Lei, Z. (2014). Psychological Safety: The History, Renaissance, and Future of an Interpersonal Construct. *Annual Review of Organizational Psychology and Organizational Behavior, 1*(1), 23–43. https://doi.org/10.1146/annurev-orgpsych-031413-091305

Greene, R. (with Elffers, J.). (2000). *The 48 Laws of Power*. Penguin Publishing Group.

Greenwald, G., MacAskill, E., & Poitras, L. (2013, June 11). Edward Snowden: The whistle-blower behind the NSA surveillance revelations. *The Guardian*. https://www.theguardian.com/world/2013/jun/09/edward-snowden-nsa-whistleblower-surveillance

Guo, F., Xue, Z., He, J., & Yasmin, F. (2023). Ethical leadership and workplace behavior in the education sector: The implications of employees' ethical work behavior. *Frontiers in Psychology, 13*, 1040000. https://doi.org/10.3389/fpsyg.2022.1040000

Hamilton, A. (2025, May 27). *It's about Damn Time: How to Turn Being Underestimated Into Your Greatest Advantage*. Porchlight Book Company. https://www.porchlightbooks.com/products/its-about-damn-time-arlan-hamilton-9780593442708

Hunt, V., Prince, S., Dixon-Fyle, S., & Yee, L. (2020). Diversity wins: How inclusion matters. *McKinsey & Company*.

Isaac, M. (2017, June 21). Uber Founder Travis Kalanick Resigns as C.E.O. *The New York Times*. https://www.nytimes.com/2017/06/21/technology/uber-ceo-travis-kalanick.html

King, C. (2024, October 4). *Yvon Chouinard: The Founder of Patagonia*. https://sustainabilitymag.com/articles/yvon-chouinard-the-founder-of-patagonia

Leggett, T. (2014, June 30). How Ford's Alan Mulally turned around its fortunes. *BBC News*. https://www.bbc.com/news/business-28087325

Leroy, H., Palanski, M. E., & Simons, T. (2012). Authentic Leadership and Behavioral Integrity as Drivers of Follower Commitment and Performance. *Journal of Business Ethics, 107*(3), 255–264. https://doi.org/10.1007/s10551-011-1036-1

Lopez, J. (2013, December 6). *The Legacy of Nelson Mandela | GW Today | The George Washington University*. GW Today. https://gwtoday.gwu.edu/legacy-nelson-mandela

Lorenzo, R., Tsusaka, M., Voigt, N., Krentz, M., & Abouzahr, K. (2018, January). *How Diverse Leadership Teams Boost Innovation*. Boston Consulting Group. https://www.bcg.com/publications/2018/how-diverse-leadership-teams-boost-innovation

Mercer, P. (2019, March 21). Christchurch shootings: New Zealand to ban military style weapons. *BBC News*. https://www.bbc.com/news/world-asia-47648549

Nadella, S., Shaw, G., & Nichols, J. T. (with Bill Gates). (2018). *Hit refresh: The quest to rediscover Microsoft's soul and imagine a better future for everyone*. Harper Collins Publishers.

NewsHour, -Dr Howard Markel Dr Howard Markel writes a monthly column for the PBS, Medicine, highlighting momentous historical events that continue to shape modern medicine H. is the director of the C. for the H. of, Michigan, the G. E. W. D. P. of the H. of M. at the U. of, Franklin, the author of "The S. of L. R., Watson, J., Crick, F., & Helix", the D. of D. D. (2014, September 29). *How the Tylenol murders of 1982 changed the way we consume medication*. PBS News. https://www.pbs.org/newshour/health/tylenol-murders-1982

Pretty, N. (2024, December 1). *Project Aristotle: Google's Data-Driven Insights on High-Performing Teams*.Aristotle Performance. https://www.aristotleperformance.com/post/project-aristotle-google-s-data-driven-insights-on-high-performing-teams

Ramadhan, D. A. (2025). The impact of authentic leadership on employee engagement through employee-organization relations. *International Journal of Emerging Research and Review*, 3(1), 1–15. https://doi.org/10.56707/ijoerar.v3i1.100

Rego, A., Sousa, M., Marques, C., & Cunha, M. (2012). Authentic leadership promoting employees' psychological capital and creativity. *Journal of Business Research*, *65*, 429–437. https://doi.org/10.1016/j.jbusres.2011.10.003

Taylor, P. (2014, June 9). *GO WITH THE FLOW*. Sports Illustrated Vault | SI.Com. https://vault.si.com/vault/2014/06/09/go-with-the-flow

Williams, J. (2021). *Bias interrupted: Creating inclusion for real and for good*. Harvard Business Review Press.

About the Author

Mitch Hayes is a business leader and operator who has built high-performing teams by leading with trust, clarity, and authenticity. He is the current CEO of Zone 4 and former President of Kardex Solutions, where he scaled the business from one employee to more than eighty and from zero revenue to more than forty million dollars in less than four years. His leadership approach helped transform the organization into a recognized partner in the warehouse automation and operations sector.

Mitch has spent his career working in environments where alignment, communication, and execution directly determine success. His experience ranges from project management to executive leadership, giving him a grounded understanding of the challenges leaders face at every level. He has coached teams through rapid growth, culture change, and difficult transitions. He has seen firsthand how authenticity enables better decisions, stronger relationships, and long-term results.

Mitch speaks to business leaders, executives, and operators about trust-based leadership and practical behaviors that create commitment, engagement, and resilience. He writes about leadership, communication, and culture on LinkedIn and is committed to helping leaders show up consistently, communicate honestly, and lead with conviction.

He lives in Cincinnati, Ohio, with his family.

https://www.linkedin.com/in/whoismitchhayes

www.ingramcontent.com/pod-product-compliance
Lightning Source LLC
LaVergne TN
LVHW100528110826
845146LV00002B/811

* 9 7 9 8 2 3 4 0 4 5 8 5 0 *